THE ZEN TEACHING OF HUANG PO

The Zen Teaching of Huang Po

ON THE TRANSMISSION OF MIND

*Being the Teaching of the Zen Master
Huang Po as recorded by the scholar
P'ei Hsiu of the T'ang Dynasty*

Rendered into English by

JOHN BLOFELD
(Chu Ch'an)

A complete translation of the Huang Po Chu'an Hsiu
Fa Yao, *including the previously unpublished* Wan Ling
Record *containing dialogues, sermons, and anecdotes*

GROVE PRESS, INC. NEW YORK

Zen Buddhism

MANUFACTURED IN THE UNITED STATES OF AMERICA

DISTRIBUTED BY RANDOM HOUSE, INC., NEW YORK

GROVE PRESS, INC., 53 EAST 11TH STREET, NEW YORK, NEW YORK 10003

CONTENTS

TRANSLATOR'S INTRODUCTION

THE TEXT

The present volume is a complete translation of the *Huang Po Ch'uan Hsin Fa Yao*, a ninth-century Chinese Buddhist text, much of which now appears in English for the first time. It contains a concise account of the sublime teachings of a great Master of the Dhyāna Sect, to which, in accordance with current Western practice, I shall henceforth refer by its Japanese name of Zen. Zen is often regarded as a uniquely Far Eastern development of Buddhism, but Zen followers claim that their Doctrine stems directly from Gautama Buddha himself. This text, which is one of the principle Zen works, follows closely the teachings proclaimed in the *Diamond Sūtra* or *Jewel of Transcendental Wisdom*, which has been ably translated by Arnold Price and published by the Buddhist Society, London. It is also close in spirit to *The Sūtra of Wei Lang (Hui Nêng)*, another of the Buddhist Society's publications. But I have been deeply struck by the astonishing similarity to our text in spirit and terminology of the not-so-Far Eastern, eighth-century *Tibetan Book of the Great Liberation*, edited by Evans-Wentz and published by the Oxford University Press. In my opinion, these four books are among the most brilliant expositions of the highest Wisdom which have so far appeared in our language; and, of them all, the present text and the *Tibetan Book of the Great Liberation* present the Doctrine in a form best suited to the needs of Western readers.

THE PLACE OF THIS TEXT IN BUDDHISM

Zen is a branch of the great Mahāyāna School prevailing in China and the more northerly countries of Eastern Asia, so its teachings are not accepted as orthodox Buddhism by followers of Hīnayāna or the Southern School. However, Western scholars are no longer unanimous in regarding Hīnayāna as being the sole guardian of the truths proclaimed by Buddhism's illustrious Founder, despite the early date of Hīnayāna's principal texts. The division into two schools took place some two thousand years ago in Northern India, since when Mahāyānists have accepted the teachings of the sister school as PART of the true Doctrine; though the latter, with less tolerance, repudiates whatever doctrines are specifically Mahāyāna. Zen, which appeared in the open much later, submits that, while all Buddhist sects present the truth in varying degrees, Zen alone preserves the very highest teachings of all—teachings based on a mysterious transmission of Mind which took place between Gautama Buddha and Mahākāśyapa, the only one of his disciples capable of receiving this transmission. Opinions as to the truth of this story naturally vary, but Masters like Huang Po obviously speak from some deep inner experience. He and his followers were concerned solely with a direct perception of truth and cannot have been even faintly interested in arguments about the historical orthodoxy of their beliefs. The great mystics of the world, such as Plotinus and Ekhart, who have plumbed the depths of consciousness and come face to face with the Inner Light, the all-pervading Silence, are so close to being unanimous concerning their experience of Reality that I, personally, am left in no doubt as to the truth of their accounts. Huang Po, in his more nearly everyday language, is clearly describing the same experience as theirs, and I assume that Gautama Buddha's mystical Enlightenment beneath the Bo Tree did not differ from theirs, unless PERHAPS in intensity and in its utter completeness. Could one suppose otherwise, one would have to accept several forms of absolute truth! Or else one would be driven to believe that some or all of these Masters were lost in clouds of self-deception. So, however slender the evidence for Zen's claim to have been founded by Gautama Buddha himself, I do not for one moment doubt that Huang Po was expressing in his own way the same experience of Eternal Truth which Gautama Buddha and others, Buddhist and non-Buddhist, have expressed in theirs. Moreover, since first embarking on the translation of this text, I have been astonished by its very close similarity to the teaching contained in the *Tibetan Book of the Great Liberation* which is attributed to the Lotus-Born Padma Sambhava. Since both are approximately of the same date, I suppose they COULD have derived from the same literary or oral source, but it seems much more probable that the two texts embody two different people's intimate perceptions of eternal truth. However, there are many who regard things otherwise and, in any case, it is proper for me to give some account of the traditional origin of Zen and of the modern theories concerning it.

9

The Origin, Growth and Expansion of Zen (Dhyāna) Buddhism

Traditional Origin

Gautama Buddha is said to have modified the exposition of his Doctrine to suit the different capacities of his various disciples and of those others who listened to his discourses. Once, at the end of a sermon, he picked a flower and held it up for the assembled monks to see. Mahākāşyapa, who alone understood the profound meaning of this gesture, responded with a smile. Later the Buddha called this disciple to him in private and mystically transmitted to him the wordless doctrine, or 'with Mind transmitted Mind'. Mahākāşyapa, in his turn, mystically transmitted the Doctrine to Ānanda, who thus became second in the line of twenty-eight Indian Patriarchs. The last of these was Bodhidharma, who travelled to China in the sixth century A.D. Here he became the First of the Chinese Patriarchs, who continued the transmission down to Hui Nêng (Wei Lang), the Sixth and last. Divisions within the sect followed and no more Patriarchs were created.

Theories Concerning the Origin and Development of the Sect

Buddhism, officially introduced into China in A.D. 61, probably reached the coast of Shantung as early as the first or second century B.C. Hīnayāna did not survive there for long, but Mahāyāna flourished exceedingly; various sects of Indian origin were developed and new sects created. One of the latest sects to appear was Zen, which rapidly attained great influence. Though an Indian origin was claimed for it, many people have doubted the truth of this; and some have gone so far as to doubt the existence of Bodhidharma himself. If, as I prefer to think, there was really such a person, he probably came to China from South India by way of Canton and visited the rulers of two Chinese states—for China was then divided, as so often in her long history.

Professor Daisetz Suzuki accepts the existence of Bodhidharma, but suggests that his teachings were derived from the Laṅkāvatāra Sūtra, which appears to contain the germs of the wordless doctrine. Dr. Hu Shih accepts neither the historical reality of Bodhidharma nor the authenticity of the earlier Zen works, regarding even the famous Sūtra of Hui Nêng (Wei Lang), the Sixth Patriarch, as a forgery of later date. To support his contentions, he adduces several eighth-century manuscripts discovered fairly recently in the Tun Huang caves, which differ both in name and substance from the traditionally accepted works of the Zen Masters. Dr. Hu Shih even describes Zen as a Chinese revolt against Buddhism—regarded as an alien doctrine from India.

I do not see that Zen sets itself up in opposition to other forms of Buddhism, including those whose Indian origin is more certain; for all sects regard dhyāna-practice as an important means towards Enlightenment, i.e. the practice of turning the mind towards and striving to pierce the veils of sensory perception and conceptual thought in order to arrive at an intuitive perception of reality. Zen does, however, emphasize this to the exclusion or near-exclusion of much else, and it also differs from most other sects in regarding Enlightenment as a process which finally occurs in less time than it takes to blink an eye. Thus it is a form of

Buddhism suited to those who prefer inward contemplation to the study of scriptures or to the performance of good works. Yet Zen is not unique in giving special emphasis to one particular aspect of the whole doctrine—if no one did that, there would be no sects. Moreover, Right Meditation (SAMMĀSAMĀDHI) forms the final step of the Noble Eightfold Path, which is accepted as the very foundation of Buddhism by Mahāyānists and Hīnayānists alike—and dhyāna-practice is aimed precisely at accomplishing that.

Hence, though there is very little evidence to prove or disprove the Indian origin of Zen, it does not seem to me especially unlikely that Bodhidharma did in fact arrive in China, bringing with him a doctrine of great antiquity inherited from his own teachers, a doctrine which infers that the seven preceding steps of the Noble Eightfold Path are to be regarded as preparation for the Eighth. And, if the Eighth is not held to be the outcome of the other Seven, it is difficult to understand why terms like 'Path' and 'steps' were employed.

The late Venerable T'ai Hsü, exemplifying a proper Buddhist attitude of broad tolerance, once described the various sects as so many beads strung on a single rosary. Mahāyāna Buddhists are encouraged to think for themselves and are free to choose whichever path best suits their individual requirements; the sectarian bitterness of the West is unknown in China. As the Chinese, though seldom puritanical, have generally been an abstemious people, sects chiefly emphasizing the strict observance of moral precepts—as does Hīnayāna—have seldom appealed to them, which may be one of the main reasons why the Southern School of Buddhism failed to take permanent root in China. Furthermore, Chinese intellectuals have since ancient times inclined to mild scepticism; to these people, Zen's austere 'simplicity' and virtual lack of ritualism must have made a strong appeal. In another way, too, the ground in China had been well prepared for Zen. On the one hand, centuries of Confucianism had predisposed scholars against the fine-spun metaphysical speculation in which Indian Buddhists have indulged with so much enthusiasm; on the other, the teaching of Lao Tzû, Chuang Tzû, the Taoist sages, had to a great extent anticipated Zen quietism and prepared the Chinese mind for the reception of a doctrine in many ways strikingly similar to their own. (For somewhat similar reasons, Zen has begun to appeal to those people in the West who are torn between the modern tradition of scepticism and the need for a profound doctrine which will give meaning to their existence.)

So it may be that the historical authenticity of Zen is of relatively little importance, except to a limited number of scholars. It will certainly not seem of much importance to those who see in the teachings of the Zen Masters a brilliant reflection of some valid inner realization of Truth. Zen has long flourished in China and Japan and is now beginning to develop in the West, because those who have put its teachings to a prolonged practical test have discovered that they satisfy certain deep spiritual needs.

The Zen Master Huang Po
When Hui Nêng (Wei Lang), the Sixth Patriarch, received the transmission from Mind to Mind, the Zen Sect had already split into two branches. The Northern Branch, which taught that the process of Enlightenment is gradual, flourished for a while under imperial patronage, but did not long survive. Meanwhile, the Southern Branch, with

its doctrine of Sudden Enlightenment, continued to expand and, later, to subdivide. The most important of the Sixth Patriarch's successors was Ma Tsu (Tao I) who died in A.D. 788. Huang Po, variously regarded as one or two generations junior to him, seems to have died as late as 850, after transmitting the Wordless Doctrine to I Hsüan, the founder of the great Lin Chi (Rinzai) Sect which still continues in China and flourishes widely in Japan. So Huang Po is in some sense regarded as the founder of this great Branch. Like all Chinese monks, he had several names, being known in his lifetime as Master Hsi Yün and as Master T'uan Chi; his posthumous name is taken from that of Mount Huang Po where he resided for many years. In Japan he is generally known as Obaku, which is the Japanese way of pronouncing the Chinese characters for Huang Po.

The Doctrine of Zen

Zen is already a familiar doctrine to many Western people, thanks to the comprehensive and illuminating works of Dr. Daisetz Tairo Suzuki, and to books by Western scholars, such as Mr. Christmas Humphreys' delightful *Zen Buddhism*. At first sight Zen works must seem so paradoxical as to bewilder the reader. On one page we are told that everything is indivisibly one Mind, on another that the moon is very much a moon and a tree indubitably a tree. Yet it is clear that this is not paradox for the sake of entertainment, for there are several million people who regard Zen as the most serious thing in life.

All Buddhists take Gautama Buddha's Enlightenment as their starting point and endeavour to attain to that transcendental knowledge that will bring them face to face with

Reality, thereby delivering them from rebirth into the space-time realm forever. Zen followers go further. They are not content to pursue Enlightenment through aeons of varied existences inevitably bound up with pain and ignorance, approaching with infinite slowness the Supreme Experience which Christian mystics have described as 'union with the Godhead'. They believe in the possibility of attaining Full Enlightenment both here and now through determined efforts to rise beyond conceptual thought and to grasp that Intuitive Knowledge which is the central fact of Enlightenment. Furthermore, they insist that the experience is both sudden and complete. While the striving may require years, the reward manifests itself in a flash. But to attain this reward, the practice of virtue and dispassion is insufficient. It is necessary to rise above such relative concepts as good and evil, sought and found, Enlightened and unenlightened, and all the rest.

To make this point clearer, let us consider some Christian ideas of God. God is regarded as the First Principle, uncaused and unbegat, which logically implies perfection; such a being cannot be discovered through the relativity of time and space. Then comes the concept 'God is good' which, as Christian mystics have pointed out, detracts from His perfection; for to be good implies not being evil—a limitation which inevitably destroys the unity and wholeness inseparable from perfection. This, of course, is not intended to imply that 'God is evil', or that 'God is both good and evil'. To a mystic, He is none of these things, for He transcends them all. Again, the idea of God as the creator of the universe suggests a dualism, a distinction between creator and created. This, if valid, places God on a lower level than perfection, for there can be neither unity nor wholeness where A excludes B or B excludes A.

Zen followers (who have much in common with mystics of other faiths) do not use the term 'God', being wary of its dualistic and anthropomorphic implications. They prefer to talk of 'the Absolute' or 'the One Mind', for which they employ many synonyms according to the aspect to be emphasized in relation to something finite. Thus, the word 'Buddha' is used as a synonym for the Absolute as well as in the sense of Gautama, the Enlightened One, for it is held that the two are identical. A Buddha's Enlightenment denotes an intuitive realization of his unity with the Absolute from which, after the death of his body, nothing remains to divide him even in appearance. Of the Absolute nothing whatever can be postulated; to say that it exists excludes non-existence; to say that it does not exist excludes existence. Furthermore, Zen followers hold that the Absolute, or union with the Absolute, is not something to be attained; one does not ENTER Nirvāṇa, for entrance to a place one has never left is impossible. The experience commonly called 'entering Nirvāṇa' is, in fact, an intuitive realization of that Self-nature which is the true Nature of all things. The Absolute, or Reality, is regarded as having for sentient beings two aspects. The only aspect perceptible to the unenlightened is the one in which individual phenomena have a separate though purely transitory existence within the limits of space-time. The other aspect is spaceless and timeless; moreover all opposites, all distinctions and 'entities' of every kind, are here seen to be One. Yet neither is this second aspect, alone, the highest fruit of Enlightenment, as many contemplatives suppose; it is only when both aspects are perceived and reconciled that the beholder may be regarded as truly Enlightened. Yet, from that moment, he ceases to be the beholder, for he is conscious of no division between beholding and beheld. This leads to further paradoxes, unless the use of words is abandoned altogether. It is incorrect to employ such mystical terminology as 'I dwell in the Absolute', 'The Absolute dwells in me', or 'I am penetrated by the Absolute', etc.; for, when space is transcended, the concepts of whole and part are no longer valid; the part IS the whole— I AM the Absolute, except that I am no longer 'I'. What I behold then is my real Self, which is the true nature of all things; see-er and seen are one and the same, yet there is no seeing, just as the eye cannot behold itself.

The single aim of the true Zen follower is so to train his mind that all thought-processes based on the dualism inseparable from 'ordinary' life are transcended, their place being taken by that Intuitive Knowledge which, for the first time, reveals to a man what he really is. If All is One, then knowledge of a being's true self-nature—his original Self—is equally a knowledge of all-nature, the nature of everything in the universe. Those who have actually achieved this tremendous experience, whether as Christians, Buddhists or members of other faiths, are agreed as to the impossibility of communicating it in words. They may employ words to point the way to others, but, until the latter have achieved the experience for themselves, they can have but the merest glimmer of the truth—a poor intellectual concept of something lying infinitely beyond the highest point ever reached by the human intellect.

It will now be clear that Zen Masters do not employ paradoxes from a love of cheap mystification, though they do occasionally make humorous use of them when humour seems needed. Usually, it is the utter impossibility of describing the Supreme Experience which explains the paradoxical nature of their speech. To affirm or deny is to limit; to limit is to shut out the light of truth; but, as words of some sort must be used in order to set disciples on to the right path, there naturally arises a series of paradoxes— sometimes of paradox within paradox within paradox.

It should perhaps be added that Huang Po's frequent criticisms of those Buddhists who follow the more conventional path, cultivating knowledge, good works and a compassionate heart through successive stages of existence, are not intended to call into question the value to humanity of such excellent practices. As a Buddhist, Huang Po must certainly have regarded these things as necessary for our proper conduct in daily life; indeed, we are told by P'ei Hsiu that his way of life was exalted; but he was concerned lest concepts such as virtue should lead people into dualism, and lest they should hold Enlightenment to be a gradual process attainable by other means than intuitive insight.

Huang Po's Use of the term 'The One Mind'

The text indicates that Huang Po was not entirely satisfied with his choice of the word 'Mind' to symbolize the inexpressible Reality beyond the reach of conceptual thought, for he more than once explains that the One Mind is not really MIND at all. But he had to use some term or other, and 'Mind' had often been used by his predecessors. As Mind conveys intangibility, it no doubt seemed to him a good choice, especially as the use of this term helps to make it clear that the part of a man usually regarded as an individual entity inhabiting his body is, in fact, not his property at all, but common to him and to everybody and every-thing else. (It must be remembered that, in Chinese, 'hsin' means not only 'mind', but 'heart' and, in some senses at least, 'spirit' or 'soul'—in short, the so-called REAL man, the inhabitant of the body-house.) If we prefer to substitute the word 'Absolute', which Huang Po occasionally uses himself, we must take care not to read into the text any preconceived notions as to the nature of the Absolute. And, of course, 'the One Mind' is no less misleading, unless we abandon all preconceived ideas, as Huang Po intended.

In an earlier translation of the first part of this book, I ventured to substitute 'Universal Mind' for 'the One Mind', hoping that the meaning would be clearer. However, various critics objected to this, and I have come to see that my term is liable to a different sort of misunderstanding; it is therefore no improvement on 'the One Mind', which at least has the merit of being a literal translation.

Dhyāna-Practice
The book tells us very little about the practice of what, for want of a better translation, is often called meditation or contemplation. Unfortunately both these words are mis-leading as they imply some object of meditation or of con-templation; and, if objectlessness be stipulated, then they may well be taken to lead to a blank or sleeplike trance, which is not at all the goal of Zen. Huang Po seems to have assumed that his audience knew something about this practice—as most keen Buddhists do, of course. He gives few instructions as to how to 'meditate', but he does tell us what to avoid. If, conceiving of the phenomenal world as illusion, we try to shut it out, we make a false distinction between the 'real' and the 'unreal'. So we must not shut

anything out, but try to reach the point where all distinctions are seen to be void, where nothing is seen as desirable or undesirable, existing or not existing. Yet this does not mean that we should make our minds blank, for then we should be no better than blocks of wood or lumps of stone; moreover, if we remained in this state, we should not be able to deal with the circumstances of daily life or be capable of observing the Zen precept: 'When hungry, eat.' Rather, we must cultivate dispassion, realizing that none of the attractive or unattractive attributes of things have any absolute existence.

Enlightenment, when it comes, will come in a flash. There can be no gradual, no partial, Enlightenment. The highly trained and zealous adept may be said to have prepared himself for Enlightenment, but by no means can he be regarded as partially Enlightened—just as a drop of water may get hotter and hotter and then, suddenly, boil; at no stage is it partly boiling, and, until the very moment of boiling, no qualitative change has occurred. In effect, however, we may go through three stages—two of non-Enlightenment and one of Enlightenment. To the great majority of people, the moon is the moon and the trees are trees. The next stage (not really higher than the first) is to perceive that moon and trees are not at all what they seem to be, since 'all is the One Mind'. When this stage is achieved, we have the concept of a vast uniformity in which all distinctions are void; and, to some adepts, this concept may come as an actual perception, as 'real' to them as were the moon and the trees before. It is said that, when Enlightenment really comes, the moon is again very much the moon and the trees exactly trees; but with a difference, for the Enlightened man is capable of perceiving both unity and multiplicity without the least contradiction between them!

Huang Po's Attitude Towards Other Schools and Sects of Buddhism

As this book is likely to be read by many Buddhists who belong to the Theravādin (Hīnayāna School) or to Mahāyāna sects other than Zen, some explanation is needed here to forestall possible misunderstandings. A casual glance at our text or at some other Zen works might well give the impression that non-Zen Buddhism is treated too lightly. It should be remembered that Huang Po was talking principally to people who were already firm and serious-minded Buddhists. He tells us himself that nothing written down should be understood out of its context or without regard to the circumstances under which the recorded sermon was given. I feel that had he been speaking to non-Buddhists, his references to the 'Three Vehicles' would have been couched in different language. A careful study of this work has persuaded me that Huang Po felt no desire to belittle the virtue of those Buddhists who disagreed with his methods, but he did feel strongly that the Zen method is productive of the fastest results. He was much concerned to show that scripture-study and the performance of good works cannot lead to Enlightenment, unless the concept-forming processes of the finite mind are brought, properly, under control. As for good works and right living, we learn from P'ei Hsiu and others that his own way of life was exalted, but he had constantly to combat the notion that good works in themselves can bring us nearer to

Enlightenment. Moreover, when the time has come for a Buddhist to discipline his mind so as to rise above duality, he enters a stage where the notions of both good and evil must be transcended like any other form of dualism. The Master was aware that many of the Buddhists he was preaching to had probably fallen into the all-too-common error of performing good works with a conscious desire to store up merit for themselves—a desire which is a form of attachment as inimical to Enlightenment as any other form of attachment. (The translator knows of several 'sincere' Buddhists who lead lives very far from noble and who indulge sometimes in actions destructive of the happiness of others, but who firmly believe that their regular offerings to the Sangha and their periodic attendance at temple services will build up enough good karma to cancel out the results of their folly and their uncharitableness to others!)

As to the study of sūtras and written works of all kinds on Buddhism, Huang Po must surely have assumed that most of the people who had taken the trouble to come to his mountain retreat for instruction were already fully conversant with Buddhist doctrine, and that what they lacked was the knowledge of mind-control. It is clear from his own words that he realized the necessity of books and teachings of various kinds for people less advanced. Unless a man is first attracted to Mysticism by the written doctrines delivered by the Lord Buddha or by other great teachers, he is most unlikely to see the necessity for mind-control, the central object of Huang Po's own teaching. Hence the Doctrine of Words must inevitably precede the Wordless Doctrine, except in certain rare cases. I am convinced that Huang Po had no intention of belittling the 'Three Vehicles'; but that, since he was talking to an audience already steeped in those teachings, he wished to emphasize that mind-control (Sammāsamādhi) is the highest teaching of all; and that without it all other practices are in vain for those who aim at gaining the mystical intuition which leads to that ineffable experience called Nirvāna.

Buddhists of other sects have often been far less charitable than Huang Po towards those sects with which—usually through ignorance—they have disagreed. Thus the Pure Land Sect or Amidism is often held up to scorn and labelled 'unBuddhist', the 'antithesis of Buddhism' and so on. This is partly because many Amidists misunderstand the teaching of their own sect, but what religion or sect would not deserve our scorn if its merits were to be judged by the popular beliefs of the general body of its followers? In fact, as I have stated in the commentary to the text, Amidism in its pure form is excellent Buddhism, for Amida Buddha symbolizes the Dharmakāya (the Buddha in the aspect of oneness with the Absolute), and entrance to the Pure Land symbolizes intuitive understanding of our own oneness with realty. Furthermore, Professor Suzuki has somewhere made the point that more Amidists achieve satori (a sudden flash of Enlightenment) than Zen adepts, because their single-minded concentration while reciting the formula 'Nāmo Amida Buddha' is an excellent form of mind-control, achievable even by simple people who have no idea of the true significance of 'Amida' and 'Pure Land'.

Another sect which comes in for much obloquy, especially from Western Buddhist writers, is that commonly known in English as Lamaism. To those who suppose that Lamaism has nothing to offer besides concessions to the superstitions of uneducated Tibetans (more than equalled by the ignorant superstitions found in more 'advanced countries'), the Oxford Tibetan Series so ably edited by Dr. Evans-Wentz provides unanswerable proof to the contrary. Huang Po's seemingly discourteous references to other sects are justified by the urgency and sincerity of his single-minded desire to emphasize the necessity for mind-control. The discourtesy exhibited by many sectarian writers would seem to have less justification.

The Division into Sermons, Dialogues and Anecdotes

The sermons alone present the doctrine in its entirety; the dialogues and anecdotes, while offering little that is new in the way of subject-matter, greatly amplify our understanding of what has gone before. This division is quite usual with Zen works. Zen Masters hold that an individual's full understanding of Zen is often precipitated by the hearing of a single phrase exactly calculated to destroy his particular demon of ignorance; so they have always favoured the brief paradoxical dialogue as a means of instruction, finding it of great value in giving a sudden jolt to a pupil's mind which may propel him towards or over the brink of Enlightenment.

Many of the dialogues recorded here took place in public assembly. We must not suppose that the erudite and accomplished P'ei Hsiu asked all the questions himself; for some of them indicate a mediocrity of understanding unworthy of that great scholar.

The Author of the Chinese Version

P'ei Hsiu was a scholar-official of great learning, whose calligraphy is still esteemed and even used as a model by students. His enthusiasm for knowledge was immense. It is recorded of him that, in the intervals between his official appointments, he would sometimes shut himself up with his books for more than a year at a time. So great was his devotion to Huang Po that he presented him with his own son as a novice, and it is known that this young man lived to become a Zen Master of standing.

The Translation

The present translation of Part I differs slightly from one I made several years ago, which was published under the title of *The Huang Po Doctrine of Universal Mind*; while Part II is now published for the first time. Words tacitly implied in the original or added for the sake of good English have not been confined in brackets, so to some extent the translation is interpretive, but the sense is strictly that of the original, unless errors have occurred in my understanding of it. These probable errors, for which I now apologize, are due to the extreme terseness of the Chinese text and to the multiplicity of meanings attached to certain Chinese characters. Thus 'hsin' may mean 'Mind' or 'mind' or 'thought', of which the last is, according to Huang Po, a major obstacle in the way of our understanding the first. Similarly, 'fa' (dharma) may mean the Doctrine, a single aspect of the Doctrine, a principle, a law, method, idea, thing, or entity of any sort whatever. Moreover, the text is highly colloquial in places and, here and there, employs a sort of T'ang Dynasty slang, the meaning of which has to be guessed from the context. When I have referred obscure passages to Chinese scholars, I have been given such a wide variety of different explanations that I have not known which to choose. In spite of all this, I believe that my rendering is on the whole faithful and that, at least, I have nowhere departed from the spirit of the teaching. The division into numbered paragraphs is my own.

I am indebted to Mr. Ting Fu Pao's Chinese *Buddhist Dictionary*, to the *Dictionary of Buddhist Terms* compiled by Soothill and Hodous, to several Chinese monks and laymen, and most of all to my wife who helped greatly in the preparation of the typescript. It is a Chinese custom to offer the merit accruing from the publication of a Buddhist work to somebody else, and this I gladly offer to my wife, Meifang. I fear, however, that Huang Po would have laughed in my face and perhaps delivered one of his famous blows if I had spoken to him of 'gaining merit' in this way!

JOHN BLOFELD (CHU CH'AN)

The Bamboo Studio, Bangkok
   October, 1957.

P'EI HSIU'S PREFACE

The great Zen Master Hsi Yün lived below the Vulture Peak on Mount Huang Po,[1] in the district of Kao An which forms part of the prefecture of Hung Chou.[2] He was third in the direct line of descent from Hui Nêng,[3] the Sixth Patriarch, and the pupil of a fellow-disciple of Hui Hai. Holding in esteem only the intuitive method of the Highest Vehicle, which cannot be communicated in words, he taught nothing but the doctrine of the One Mind; holding that there is nothing else to teach, in that both mind and substance are void and that the chain of causation is motionless. Mind is like the sun journeying through the sky and emitting glorious light uncontaminated by the finest particle of dust. To those who have realized the nature of Reality, there is nothing old or new, and conceptions of shallowness and depth are meaningless. Those who speak of it do not attempt to explain it, establish no sects and open no doors or windows. That which is before you is it. Begin to reason about it and you will at once fall into error. Only when you have understood this will you perceive your oneness with the original Buddha-nature. Therefore his words were simple, his reasoning direct, his way of life exalted and his habits unlike the habits of other men.

[1] From which he takes his posthumous name.
[2] In the modern province of Kiangsi.
[3] Wei Lang.

27

Disciples hastened to him from all quarters, looking up to him as to a lofty mountain, and through their contact with him awoke to Reality. Of the crowds which flocked to see him, there were always more than a thousand with him at a time.

In the second year of Hui Ch'ang (A.D. 843), when I was in charge of the district of Chung Lin, I welcomed him on his coming to that city from the mountain where he resided. We stayed together in the Lung Hsing Monastery where, day and night, I questioned him about the Way. Moreover, in the second year of T'ai Chung (A.D. 849), while governing the district of Wan Ling, I again had occasion to welcome him ceremoniously to the place where I was stationed. This time we stayed quietly at the K'ai Yuan Monastery, where also I studied under him day and night. After leaving him, I recorded what I had learnt and, though able to set down only about a fifth of it, I esteem it as a direct transmission of the Doctrine. At first I was diffident about publishing what I had written; but now, fearing that these vital and penetrating teachings will be lost to future generations, I have done so. Moreover, I gave the manuscript to the monks T'ai Chou and Fa Chien, requesting them to return to the Kuang T'ang Monastery on the old mountain[1] and to ask the elder monks there how far it agrees with what they themselves used frequently to hear in the past.

Written on the eighth day of the tenth moon of the eleventh year of T'ai Chung (A.D. 858) of the T'ang Dynasty.

[1] Mount Huang Po.

PART ONE

THE CHÜN CHOU RECORD OF THE ZEN MASTER HUANG PO (TUAN CHI)

A collection of sermons and dialogues recorded by P'ei Hsiu while in the city of Chün Chou

1. The Master said to me: All the Buddhas and all sentient beings are nothing but the One Mind, beside which nothing exists. This Mind, which is without beginning, is unborn[1] and indestructible. It is not green nor yellow, and has neither form nor appearance. It does not belong to the categories of things which exist or do not exist, nor can it be thought of in terms of new or old. It is neither long nor short, big nor small, for it transcends all limits, measures, names, traces and comparisons. It is that which you see before you—begin to reason about it and you at once fall into error. It is like the boundless void which cannot be fathomed or measured. The One Mind alone is the Buddha, and there is no distinction between the Buddha and sentient things, but that sentient beings are attached to forms and so seek externally for Buddhahood. By their very seeking they lose it, for that is using the Buddha to seek for the Buddha and using mind to grasp Mind. Even

---

[1] Unborn, not in the sense of eternity, for this allows contrast with its opposite; but unborn in the sense that it belongs to no categories admitting of alteration or antithesis.

though they do their utmost for a full aeon, they will not be able to attain to it. They do not know that, if they put a stop to conceptual thought and forget their anxiety, the Buddha will appear before them, for this Mind is the Buddha and the Buddha is all living beings. It is not the less for being manifested in ordinary beings, nor is it greater for being manifested in the Buddhas.

*   *   *

2. As to performing the six pāramitās[1] and vast numbers of similar practices, or gaining merits as countless as the sands of the Ganges, since you are fundamentally complete in every respect, you should not try to supplement that perfection by such meaningless practices. When there is occasion for them, perform them; and, when the occasion is passed, remain quiescent. If you are not absolutely convinced that the Mind is the Buddha, and if you are attached to forms, practices and meritorious performances, your way of thinking is false and quite incompatible with the Way. The Mind is the Buddha, nor are there any other Buddhas or any other mind. It is bright and spotless as the void, having no form or appearance whatever. To make use of your minds to think conceptually is to leave the substance and attach yourselves to form. The Ever-Existent Buddha is not a Buddha of form or attachment. To practise the six pāramitās and a myriad similar practices with the intention of becoming a Buddha thereby is to advance by stages, but the Ever-Existent Buddha is not a Buddha of stages. Only awake to the One Mind, and there is nothing whatsoever to be attained. This is the REAL Buddha. The

[1] Charity, morality, patience under affliction, zealous application, right control of mind and the application of the highest wisdom.

Buddha and all sentient beings are the One Mind and nothing else.

*　　　*　　　*

3. Mind is like the void in which there is no confusion or evil, as when the sun wheels through it shining upon the four corners of the world. For, when the sun rises and illuminates the whole earth, the void gains not in brilliance; and, when the sun sets, the void does not darken. The phenomena of light and dark alternate with each other, but the nature of the void remains unchanged. So it is with the Mind of the Buddha and of sentient beings. If you look upon the Buddha as presenting a pure, bright or Enlightened appearance, or upon sentient beings as presenting a foul, dark or mortal-seeming appearance, these conceptions resulting from attachment to form will keep you from supreme knowledge, even after the passing of as many aeons as there are sands in the Ganges. There is only the One Mind and not a particle of anything else on which to lay hold, for this Mind is the Buddha. If you students of the Way do not awake to this Mind substance, you will overlay Mind with conceptual thought, you will seek the Buddha outside yourselves, and you will remain attached to forms, pious practices and so on, all of which are harmful and not at all the way to supreme knowledge.

*　　　*　　　*

4. Making offerings to all the Buddhas of the universe is not equal to making offerings to one follower of the Way who has eliminated conceptual thought. Why? Because such a one forms no concepts whatever. The substance of the Absolute is inwardly like wood or stone, in that it is

motionless, and outwardly like the void, in that it is without bounds or obstructions. It is neither subjective nor objective, has no specific location, is formless, and cannot vanish. Those who hasten towards it dare not enter, fearing to hurtle down through the void with nothing to cling to or to stay their fall. So they look to the brink and retreat. This refers to all those who seek such a goal through cognition. Thus, those who seek the goal through cognition are like the fur (*many*), while those who obtain intuitive knowledge of the Way are like the horns (*few*).[1]

*   *   *

5. Mañjuśrī represents fundamental law and Samantabhadra, activity. By the former is meant the law of the real and unbounded void, and by the latter the inexhaustible activities beyond the sphere of form. Avalokiteśvara represents boundless compassion; Mahāsthāma, great wisdom, and Vimalakīrti, spotless name.[2] Spotless refers to the real nature of things, while name means form; yet form is really one with real nature, hence the combined term 'spotless name'.[3] All the qualities typified by the great Bodhisattvas are inherent in men and are not to be separated from the One Mind. Awake to it, and it is there. You students of the Way who do not awake to this in your own

---

[1] Compare this with Professor Suzuki's: 'That which is known as mind in discursive reasoning is no-mind, though without this Mind cannot be reached.'

[2] This abstract notion of the Bodhisattvas, regarded by some sects as individual spiritual entities, is shared by some Buddhists outside the Zen Sect.

[3] Zen teaches that, though the phenomenal world based on sensory experience has only relative existence, it is wrong to regard it as something separate from the One Mind. It is the One Mind wrongly apprehended. As the Hṛidaya Sūtra says: 'Form is not different from void, void from form; form is void and void is form.'

minds, and who are attached to appearances or who seek for something objective outside your own minds, have all turned your backs on the Way. The sands of the Ganges! The Buddha said of these sands: 'If all the Buddhas and Bodhisattvas with Indra and all the gods walk across them, the sands do not rejoice; and, if oxen, sheep, reptiles and insects tread upon them, the sands are not angered. For jewels and perfumes they have no longing, and for the stinking filth of manure and urine they have no loathing.'

*   *   *

6. This Mind is no mind of conceptual thought and it is completely detached from form. So Buddhas and sentient beings do not differ at all. If you can only rid yourselves of conceptual thought, you will have accomplished everything. But if you students of the Way do not rid yourselves of conceptual thought in a flash, even though you strive for aeon after aeon, you will never accomplish it. Enmeshed in the meritorious practices of the Three Vehicles, you will be unable to attain Enlightenment. Nevertheless, the realization of the One Mind may come after a shorter or a longer period. There are those who, upon hearing this teaching, rid themselves of conceptual thought in a flash. There are others who do this after following through the Ten Beliefs, the Ten Stages, the Ten Activities and the Ten Bestowals of Merit. Yet others accomplish it after passing through the Ten Stages of a Bodhisattva's Progress.[1] But

[1] These various categories of ten are all part of the doctrine as taught by certain other sects. Huang Po wishes to make it clear that, though these may be useful in preparing the ground, the mind must in any case take a sudden leap, and that having passed through these stages in nowise constitutes partial Enlightenment.

whether they transcend conceptual thought by a longer or a shorter way, the result is a state of BEING: there is no pious practising and no action of realizing. That there is nothing which can be attained is not idle talk; it is the truth. Moreover, whether you accomplish your aim in a single flash of thought or after going through the Ten Stages of a Bodhisattva's Progress, the achievement will be the same; for this state of being admits of no degrees, so the latter method merely entails aeons of unnecessary suffering and toil.[1]

*   *   *

7. The building up of good and evil both involve attachment to form.[2] Those who, being attached to form, do evil have to undergo various incarnations unnecessarily; while those who, being attached to form, do good, subject themselves to toil and privation equally to no purpose. In either case it is better to achieve sudden self-realization and to grasp the fundamental Dharma. This Dharma is Mind, beyond which there is no Dharma; and this Mind is the Dharma, beyond which there is no mind. Mind in itself is not mind, yet neither is it no-mind. To say that Mind is no-mind implies something existent.[3] Let there be a silent understanding and no more. Away with all thinking and explaining. Then we may say that the Way of Words has

---

[1] Merit, however excellent in itself, has nothing to do with Enlightenment.

[2] According to Zen, virtuous actions should be performed by adepts, but not with a view to accumulating merit and not as a means to Enlightenment. The door should remain perfectly unattached to the actions and to their results.

[3] In other words, Mind is an arbitary term for something that cannot properly be expressed in words.

been cut off and movements of the mind eliminated. This Mind is the pure Buddha-Source inherent in all men. All wriggling beings possessed of sentient life and all the Buddhas and Bodhisattvas are of this one substance and do not differ. Differences arise from wrong-thinking only and lead to the creation of all kinds of karma.[1]

*   *   *

8. Our original Buddha-Nature is, in highest truth, devoid of any atom of objectivity. It is void, omnipresent, silent, pure; it is glorious and mysterious peaceful joy—and that is all. Enter deeply into it by awaking to it yourself. That which is before you is it, in all its fullness, utterly complete. There is naught beside. Even if you go through all the stages of a Bodhisattva's progress towards Buddhahood, one by one; when at last, in a single flash, you attain to full realization, you will only be realizing the Buddha-Nature which has been with you all the time; and by all the foregoing stages you will have added to it nothing at all.[2] You will come to look upon those aeons of work and achievement as no better than unreal actions performed in a dream. That is why the Tathāgata said: 'I truly attained nothing from complete, unexcelled Enlightenment. Had there been anything attained, Dīpamkara Buddha would not have

[1] Karma, even good karma, leads to rebirth and prolongs the wanderings of the supposedly individual entity; for when good karma has worked itself out in consequent enjoyment, the 'individual' is as far from understanding the One Mind as ever.

[2] Enlightenment must come in a flash, whether you have passed through the preliminary stages or not, so the latter can well be dispensed with, except that, for reasons unconnected with Enlightenment, Zen requires of adepts an attitude of kindness and helpfulness towards all living creatures.

made the prophecy concerning me.'[1] He also said: 'This Dharma is absolutely without distinctions, neither high nor low, and its name is Bodhi.' It is pure Mind, which is the source of everything and which, whether appearing as sentient beings or as Buddhas, as the rivers and mountains of the world which has form, as that which is formless, or as penetrating the whole universe, is absolutely without distinctions, there being no such entities as selfness and otherness.

*   *   *

9. This pure Mind, the source of everything, shines forever and on all with the brilliance of its own perfection. But the people of the world do not awake to it, regarding only that which sees, hears, feels and knows as mind. Blinded by their own sight, hearing, feeling and knowing, they do not perceive the spiritual brilliance of the source-substance. If they would only eliminate all conceptual thought in a flash, that source-substance would manifest itself like the sun ascending through the void and illuminating the whole universe without hindrance or bounds. Therefore, if you students of the Way seek to progress through seeing, hearing, feeling and knowing, when you are deprived of your perceptions, your way to Mind will be cut off and you will find nowhere to enter. Only realize that, though real Mind

---

[1] This quotation refers to the Diamond Sūtra, as do many of the others either directly or indirectly. Dīpaṃkara Buddha, during a former life of Gautama Buddha, prophesied that he would one day attain to Buddhahood. Huang Po means that the prophecy would not have been made if Dīpaṃkara Buddha had supposed that Gautama Buddha's Enlightenment would lead to the actual attainment of something he had not already *been* from the very first; for then Enlightenment would not have led to Buddhahood, which implies a voidness of all distinctions such as attainer, attained, non-attainer and non-attained.

is expressed in these perceptions, it neither forms part of them nor is separate from them. You should not start REASONING from these perceptions, nor allow them to give rise to conceptual thought; yet nor should you seek the One Mind apart from them or abandon them in your pursuit of the Dharma. Do not keep them nor abandon them nor dwell in them nor cleave to them. Above, below and around you, all is spontaneously existing, for there is nowhere which is outside the Buddha-Mind.

*   *   *

10. When the people of the world hear it said that the Buddhas transmit the Doctrine of the Mind, they suppose that there is something to be attained or realized apart from Mind, and thereupon they use Mind to seek the Dharma, not knowing that Mind and the object of their search are one. Mind cannot be used to seek something from Mind; for then, after the passing of millions of aeons, the day of success will still not have dawned. Such a method is not to be compared with suddenly eliminating conceptual thought, which is the fundamental Dharma. Suppose a warrior, forgetting that he was already wearing his pearl on his forehead, were to seek for it elsewhere, he could travel the whole world without finding it. But if someone who knew what was wrong were to point it out to him, the warrior would immediately realize that the pearl had been there all the time. So, if you students of the Way are mistaken about your own real Mind, not recognizing that it is the Buddha, you will consequently look for him elsewhere, indulging in various achievements and practices and expecting to attain realization by such graduated practices.

But, even after aeons of diligent searching, you will not be able to attain to the Way. These methods cannot be compared to the sudden elimination of conceptual thought, in the certain knowledge that there is nothing at all which has absolute existence, nothing on which to lay hold, nothing on which to rely, nothing in which to abide, nothing subjective or objective. It is by preventing the rise of conceptual thought that you will realize Bodhi; and, when you do, you will just be realizing the Buddha who has always existed in your own Mind! Aeons of striving will prove to be so much wasted effort; just as, when the warrior found his pearl, he merely discovered what had been hanging on his forehead all the time; and just as his finding of it had nothing to do with his efforts to discover it elsewhere. Therefore the Buddha said: 'I truly attained nothing from complete, unexcelled Enlightenment.' It was for fear that people would not believe this that he drew upon what is seen with the five sorts of vision and spoken with the five kinds of speech. So this quotation is by no means empty talk, but expresses the highest truth.

*   *   *

11. Students of the Way should be sure that the four elements composing the body do not constitute the 'self', that the 'self' is not an entity; and that it can be deduced from this that the body is neither 'self' nor entity. Moreover, the five aggregates composing the mind (*in the common sense*) do not constitute either a 'self' or an entity ; hence, it can be deduced that the (*so-called individual*) mind is neither 'self' nor entity. The six sense organs (*including the brain*) which, together with their six types of perception and the

six kinds of objects of perception, constitute the sensory world, must be understood in the same way. Those eighteen aspects of sense are separately and together void. There is only Mind-Source, limitless in extent and of absolute purity.

*   *   *

12. Thus, there is sensual eating and wise eating. When the body composed of the four elements suffers the pangs of hunger and accordingly you provide it with food, but without greed, that is called wise eating. On the other hand, if you gluttonously delight in purity and flavour, you are permitting the distinctions which arise from wrong thinking. Merely seeking to gratify the organ of taste without realizing when you have taken enough is called sensual eating.[1]

*   *   *

13. Śrāvakas reach Enlightenment by hearing the Dharma, so they are called Śrāvakas.[2] Śrāvakas do not comprehend their own mind, but allow concepts to arise from listening to the doctrine. Whether they hear of the existence of Bodhi and Nirvāṇa through supernormal powers or good fortune or preaching, they will attain to Buddhahood only

[1] This is a simple example of the wrong use of the six senses. Of course we must use them for dealing with the world as it affects our daily lives, but our employment of them should be limited to what is strictly necessary for our wellbeing.

[2] Huang Po sometimes stretches this term to apply to Hīnayānists in general. The literal meaning of its Chinese equivalent is 'those who hear' and Huang Po implies that Hīnayānists pay too much attention to the literal meaning of the Scriptures, instead of seeking intuitive knowledge through eliminating conceptual thought. Those able to apply the latter method have no need of scriptures.

after three aeons of infinitely long duration. All these belong to the way of the Śrāvakas, so they are called Śrāvaka-Buddhas. But to awaken suddenly to the fact that your own Mind is the Buddha, that there is nothing to be attained or a single action to be performed—this is the Supreme Way; this is really to be as a Buddha. It is only to be feared that you students of the Way, by the coming into existence of a single thought, may raise a barrier between yourselves and the Way. From thought-instant to thought-instant, no FORM; from thought-instant to thought-instant, no ACTIVITY—that is to be a Buddha! If you students of the Way wish to become Buddhas, you need study no doctrines whatever, but learn only how to avoid seeking for and attaching yourselves to anything. Where nothing is sought this implies Mind unborn; where no attachment exists, this implies Mind not destroyed; and that which is neither born nor destroyed is the Buddha. The eighty-four thousand methods for countering the eighty-four thousand forms of delusion are merely figures of speech for drawing people towards the Gate. In fact, none of them have real existence. Relinquishment of every-thing is the Dharma, and he who understands this is a Buddha, but the relinquishment of ALL delusions leaves no Dharma on which to lay hold.[1]

*   *   *

14. If you students of the Way desire knowledge of this great mystery, only avoid attachment to any single thing

[1] Buddhists of most sects are taught to relinquish sensual attachments and to cling singlemindedly to the Dharma. Huang Po goes further in showing that any form of attachment, even attachment to the Dharma, leads us away from the truth.

beyond Mind. To say that the real Dharmakāya of the Buddha[1] resembles the Void is another way of saying that the Dharmakāya is the Void and that the Void is the Dharmakāya. People often claim that the Dharmakāya is in the Void and that the Void contains the Dharmakāya, not realizing that they are one and the same. But if you define the Void as something existing, then it is not the Dharmakāya; and if you define the Dharmakāya as something existing, then it is not the Void. Only refrain from any objective conception of the Void; then it is the Dharmakāya: and, if only you refrain from any objective conception of the Dharmakāya, why, then it is the Void. These two do not differ from each other, nor is there any difference between sentient beings and Buddhas, or between saṁsāra and Nirvāṇa, or between delusion and Bodhi. When all such forms are abandoned, there is the Buddha. Ordinary people look to their surroundings, while followers of the Way look to Mind, but the true Dharma is to forget them both. The former is easy enough, the latter very difficult. Men are afraid to forget their minds, fearing to fall through the Void with nothing to stay their fall. They do not know that the Void is not really void, but the realm of the real Dharma. This spiritually enlightening nature is without beginning, as ancient as the Void, subject neither to birth nor to destruction, neither existing nor not existing, neither impure nor pure, neither clamorous nor silent, neither old nor young, occupying no space, having neither inside nor outside, size nor form, colour nor sound. It cannot be looked for or sought, comprehended by wisdom or knowledge, explained in words, contacted materially or reached by meritorious achievement. All the Buddhas and

[1] The highest of the three Bodies, synonymous with the Absolute.

Bodhisattvas, together with all wriggling things possessed of life, share in this great Nirvāṇic nature. This nature is Mind; Mind is the Buddha, and the Buddha is the Dharma. Any thought apart from this truth is entirely a wrong thought. You cannot use Mind to seek Mind, the Buddha to seek the Buddha, or the Dharma to seek the Dharma. So you students of the Way should immediately refrain from conceptual thought. Let a tacit understanding be all! Any mental process must lead to error. There is just a transmission of Mind with Mind. This is the proper view to hold. Be careful not to look outwards to material surroundings. To mistake material surroundings for Mind is to mistake a thief for your son.[1]

*　　　　*　　　　*

15. It is only in contradistinction to greed, anger and ignorance that abstinence, calm and wisdom exist. Without illusion, how could there be Enlightenment? Therefore Bodhidharma said: 'The Buddha enunciated all Dharmas in order to eliminate every vestige of conceptual thinking. If I refrained entirely from conceptual thought, what would be the use of all the Dharmas?' Attach yourselves to nothing beyond the pure Buddha-Nature which is the original source of all things. Suppose you were to adorn the Void with countless jewels, how could they remain in position? The Buddha-Nature is like the Void; though you were to adorn it with inestimable merit and wisdom, how could

[1] There is a story of a man who mistook a thief for his long-lost son and, giving him a warm welcome, enabled the latter to sneak away with most of his possessions. Those who place reliance on material things are in danger of losing that most valuable of all possessions—the key to the riddle of life which unlocks Nirvāna's gate.

they remain there?[1] They would only serve to conceal its original Nature and to render it invisible.

That which is called the Doctrine of Mental Origins (*followed by certain other sects*) postulates that all things are built up in Mind and that they manifest themselves upon contact with external environment, ceasing to be manifest when that environment is not present. But it is wrong to conceive of an environment separate from the pure, unvarying nature of all things.[2]

That which is called the Mirror of Concentration and Wisdom (*another reference to non-Zen Mahāyāna doctrine*) requires the use of sight, hearing, feeling and cognition, which lead to successive states of calm and agitation. But these involve conceptions based on environmental objects; they are temporary expedients appertaining to one of the lower categories of 'roots of goodness'.[3] And this category of 'roots of goodness' merely enables people to understand what is said to them. If you wish to experience Enlightenment yourselves, you must not indulge in such conceptions. They are all environmental Dharmas concerning things which are and things which are not, based on existence and non-existence. If only you will avoid concepts of existence and non-existence in regard to absolutely everything, you will then perceive THE DHARMA.

* * *

[1] Other Buddhist sects attach great importance to the acquisition of merit and wisdom, but this implies a dualistic conception of reality which Zen considers an insuperable obstacle to realization of the One Mind.

[2] This constitutes a warning against another type of dualism.

[3] Roots of goodness are believed by some Mahāyānaists to be 'Enlightenment-potentials' of varying degrees of strength with which individuals are reborn in accordance with the varying merits gained in former lives.

16. On the first day of the ninth moon, the Master said to me: From the time when the Great Master Bodhidharma arrived in China, he spoke only of the One Mind and transmitted only the one Dharma. He used the Buddha to transmit the Buddha, never speaking of any other Buddha. He used the Dharma to transmit the Dharma, never speaking of any other Dharma. That Dharma was the wordless Dharma, and that Buddha was the intangible Buddha, since they were in fact that Pure Mind which is the source of all things. This is the only truth; all else is false. Prajñā is wisdom; wisdom is the formless original Mind-Source. Ordinary people do not seek the Way, but merely indulge their six senses which lead them back into the six realms of existence. A student of the Way, by allowing himself a single saṃsāric thought, falls among devils. If he permits himself a single thought leading to differential perception, he falls into heresy. To hold that there is something born and to try to eliminate it, that is to fall among the Śrāvakas.[1] To hold that things are not born but capable of destruction is to fall among the Pratyekas.[2] Nothing is born, nothing is destroyed. Away with your dualism, your likes and dislikes. Every single thing is just the One Mind. When you have perceived this, you will have mounted the Chariot of the Buddhas.

*   *   *

17. Ordinary people all indulge in conceptual thought

---

[1] Huang Po, according to his usual custom, is using the word Śrāvaka to mean Hīnayānist. Hīnayānists are dualists in that they seek to overcome their saṃsāric life in order to enter Nirvāṇa; while Zen perceives that Saṃsāra is no other than Nirvāṇa.

[2] Huang Po customarily uses or misuses this word to mean the Mādhyamikists or followers of the Middle Vehicle.

based on environmental phenomena, hence they feel desire and hatred. To eliminate environmental phenomena, just put an end to your conceptual thinking. When this ceases, environmental phenomena are void; and when these are void, thought ceases. But if you try to eliminate environment without first putting a stop to conceptual thought, you will not succeed, but merely increase its power to disturb you. Thus all things are naught but Mind—intangible Mind; so what can you hope to attain? Those who are students of Prajñā[1] hold that there is nothing tangible whatever, so they cease thinking of the Three Vehicles.[2] There is only the one reality, neither to be realized nor attained. To say 'I am able to realize something' or 'I am able to attain something' is to place yourself among the arrogant. The men who flapped their garments and left the meeting as mentioned in the Lotus Sūtra were just such people.[3] Therefore the Buddha said: 'I truly obtained nothing from Enlightenment.' There is just a mysterious tacit understanding and no more.

*   *   *

18. If an ordinary man, when he is about to die, could only see the five elements of consciousness as void; the four physical elements as not constituting an 'I'; the real Mind as formless and neither coming nor going; his nature as something neither commencing at his birth nor perishing at his death, but as whole and motionless in its very depths; his Mind and environmental objects as one—if he could really accomplish this, he would receive Enlightenment in

[1] Here used to mean Wisdom in the sense of Zen.
[2] I.e. the Three Great Schools teaching gradual Enlightenment.
[3] These people THOUGHT they had understood and were smugly self-satisfied.

a flash. He would no longer be entangled by the Triple
World; he would be a World-Transcendor. He would be
without even the faintest tendency towards rebirth. If he
should behold the glorious sight of all the Buddhas coming
to welcome him, surrounded by every kind of gorgeous
manifestation, he would feel no desire to approach them.
If he should behold all sorts of horrific forms surrounding
him, he would experience no terror. He would just be himself, oblivious of conceptual thought and one with the
Absolute. He would have attained the state of uncon-
ditioned being. This, then, is the fundamental principle.[1]

*   *   *

19. On the eighth day of the tenth moon, the Master said
to me: That which is called the City of Illusion contains the
Two Vehicles, the Ten Stages of a Bodhisattva's Progress,
and the two forms of Full Enlightenment.[2] All of them are
powerful teachings for arousing people's interest, but they
still belong to the City of Illusion.[3] That which is called the
Place of Precious Things is the real Mind, the original
Buddha-Essence, the treasure of our own real Nature.
These jewels cannot be measured or accumulated. Yet since
there are neither Buddha nor sentient beings, neither
subject nor object, where can there be a City of Precious

[1] This paragraph is, perhaps, one of the finest expositions of Zen
teaching, for it encompasses in a few words almost the entire scope of
that vast and penetrating wisdom.
[2] Including the form which leads to the awakening of others.
[3] The City of Illusion is a term taken from the Lotus Sūtra and here
implies temporary or incomplete Nirvāna. From the point of view of
Zen, all the teachings of the many sects based on a belief in gradual
Enlightenment are likely to lead their followers to the City of Illusion,
because all of them apparently subscribe to some form or other of
dualism.

Things? If you ask, 'Well, so much for the City of Illusion, but where is the Place of Precious Things?', it is a place to which no directions can be given. For, if it could be pointed out, it would be a place existing in space; hence, it could not be the real Place of Precious Things. All we can say is that it is close by. It cannot be exactly described, but when you have a tacit understanding of its substance, it is there.

* * *

20. Icchantikas are those with beliefs which are incomplete. All beings within the six realms of existence, including those who follow Mahāyāna and Hīnayāna, if they do not believe in their potential Buddhahood, are accordingly called Icchantikas with cut-off roots of goodness. Bodhisattvas[1] who believe deeply in the Buddha-Dharma, without accepting the division into Mahāyāna and Hīnayāna, but who do not realize the one Nature of Buddhas and sentient beings, are accordingly called Icchantikas with roots of goodness. Those who are Enlightened largely through hearing the spoken doctrine are termed Śrāvakas (*hearers*). Those Enlightened through perception of the law of karma are called Pratyeka-Buddhas.[2] Those who become Buddhas, but not from Enlightenment occurring in their own minds, are called Hearer-Buddhas. Most students of the Way are Enlightened through the Dharma which is taught in words and not through the Dharma of Mind. Even after successive aeons of effort, they will not become attuned to the original Buddha-Essence. For those who

[1] Here meaning Buddhists.
[2] Commonly meaning those Buddhas who do not interest themselves in the Enlightenment of others.

are not Enlightened from within their own Mind, but from hearing the Dharma which is taught in words, make light of Mind and attach importance to doctrine, so they advance only step by step, neglecting their original Mind. Thus, if only you have a tacit understanding of Mind, you will not need to search for any Dharma, for then Mind is the Dharma.[1]

*   *   *

21. People are often hindered by environmental phenomena from perceiving Mind, and by individual events from perceiving underlying principles; so they often try to escape from environmental phenomena in order to still their minds, or to obscure events in order to retain their grasp of principles. They do not realize that this is merely to obscure phenomena with Mind, events with principles. Just let your minds become void and environmental phenomena will void themselves; let principles cease to stir and events will cease stirring of themselves.[2] Do not employ Mind in this perverted way.

Many people are afraid to empty their minds lest they may plunge into the Void. They do not know that their own Mind is the void. The ignorant eschew phenomena but not thought; the wise eschew thought but not phenomena.[3]

*   *   *

[1] Most of this paragraph is intended to make it clear that, though Buddhism of the gradual school does produce results, they take long to attain and are at least incomplete compared with results obtained through Zen.

[2] To FORCE the mind to blot out phenomena shows ignorance of the identity of the one with the other.

[3] This profound teaching is aimed partly at those Buddhists who practise a form of meditation which aims at temporarily blotting out the material world.

22. The Bodhisattva's mind is like the void, for he relinquishes everything and does not even desire to accumulate merits. There are three kinds of relinquishment. When everything inside and outside, bodily and mental, has been relinquished; when, as in the Void, no attachments are left; when all action is dictated purely by place and circumstance; when subjectivity and objectivity are forgotten —that is the highest form of relinquishment. When, on the one hand, the Way is followed by the performance of virtuous acts; while, on the other, relinquishment of merit takes place and no hope of reward is entertained—that is the medium form of relinquishment. When all sorts of virtuous actions are performed in the hope of reward by those who, nevertheless, know of the Void by hearing the Dharma and who are therefore unattached—that is the lowest form of relinquishment. The first is like a blazing torch held to the front which makes it impossible to mistake the path; the second is like a blazing torch held to one side, so that it is sometimes light and sometimes dark; the third is like a blazing torch held behind, so that pitfalls in front are not seen.[1]

*   *   *

23. Thus, the mind of the Bodhisattva is like the Void and everything is relinquished by it. When thoughts of the past cannot be taken hold of, that is relinquishment of the past. When thoughts of the present cannot be taken hold of, that is relinquishment of the present. When thoughts of the future cannot be taken hold of, that is relinquishment of

[1] These three types of relinquishment probably refer obliquely to Zen, Mahāyāna and Hīnayāna respectively.

the future. This is called utter relinquishment of Triple Time. Since the Tathāgata entrusted Kāśyapa with the Dharma until now, Mind has been transmitted with Mind, and these Minds have been identical. A transmission of Void cannot be made through words. A transmission in concrete terms cannot be the Dharma. Thus Mind is transmitted with Mind and these Minds do not differ. Transmitting and receiving transmission are both a most difficult kind of mysterious understanding, so that few indeed have been able to receive it. In fact, however, Mind is not Mind and transmission is not really transmission.[1]

*   *   *

24. A Buddha has three bodies. By the Dharmakāya is meant the Dharma of the omnipresent voidness of the real self-existent Nature of everything. By the Sambhogakāya is meant the Dharma of the underlying universal purity of things. By the Nirmāṇakāya is meant the Dharmas of the six practices leading to Nirvāṇa and all other such devices. The Dharma of the Dharmakāya cannot be sought through speech or hearing or the written word. There is nothing which can be said or made evident. There is just the omnipresent voidness of the real self-existent Nature of everything, and no more. Therefore, saying that there is no Dharma to be explained in words is called preaching the Dharma. The Sambhogakāya and the Nirmāṇakāya both respond with appearances suited to particular circumstances. Spoken Dharmas which respond to events through the senses and in all sorts of guises are none of them the real Dharma. So it is said that the Sambhogakāya or the

[1] This is a reminder that ALL terms used in Zen are mere makeshifts.

Nirmaṇakāya is not a real Buddha or preacher of the Dharma.[1]

*   *   *

25. The term unity refers to a homogeneous spiritual brilliance which separates into six harmoniously blended 'elements'. The homogeneous spiritual brilliance is the One Mind, while the six harmoniously blended 'elements' are the six sense organs. These six sense organs become severally united with objects that defile them—the eyes with form, the ear with sound, the nose with smell, the tongue with taste, the body with touch, and the thinking mind with entities. Between these organs and their objects arise the six sensory perceptions, making eighteen sense-realms in all. If you understand that these eighteen realms have no objective existence, you will bind the six harmoniously blended 'elements' into a single spiritual brilliance—a single spiritual brilliance which is the One Mind. All students of the Way know this, but cannot avoid forming concepts of 'a single spiritual brilliance' and 'the six harmoniously blended elements'. Accordingly they are chained to entities and fail to achieve a tacit understanding of original Mind.[2]

*   *   *

[1] As usual, Huang Po is using familiar Sanskrit terms in a way peculiar to himself. Usually, the Dharmakāya means the highest aspect of a Buddha, i.e. as one with the Absolute; the Sambhogakāya is the glorified Body of a Buddha in his supramundane existence; and the Nirmāṇakāya may be any of the various transformations in which a Buddha appears in the world. In Zen, the first is absolute truth in unimaginable and perfect form, the second is the highest concept of absolute truth of which unenlightened human beings are capable—an underlying purity and unity; the third represents the various methods by which we hope to obtain perception of absolute truth.

[2] This points to those people who are capable of understanding the doctrine intelligently but who have not yet entirely succeeded in throwing off the burden of concepts.

26. When the Tathāgata manifested himself in this world, he wished to preach a single Vehicle of Truth. But people would not have believed him and, by scoffing at him, would have become immersed in the sea of sorrow (*saṁsāra*). On the other hand, if he had said nothing at all, that would have been selfishness, and he would not have been able to diffuse knowledge of the mysterious Way for the benefit of sentient beings. So he adopted the expedient of preaching that there are Three Vehicles. As, however, these Vehicles are relatively greater and lesser, unavoidably there are shallow teachings and profound teachings—none of them being the original Dharma. So it is said that there is only a One-Vehicle Way; if there were more, they could not be real. Besides there is absolutely no way of describing the Dharma of the One Mind. Therefore the Tathāgata called Kāṣyapa to come and sit with him on the Seat of Proclaiming the Law, separately entrusting to him the Wordless Dharma of the One Mind. This branchless Dharma was to be separately practised; and those who should be tacitly Enlightened would arrive at the state of Buddhahood.[1]

*　　　*　　　*

27. Q: What is the Way and how must it be followed?

A: What sort of THING do you suppose the Way to be, that you should wish to FOLLOW it?

Q: What instructions have the Masters everywhere given for dhyāna-practice and the study of the Dharma?

[1] This passage demonstrates that Huang Po himself accepted the traditional origin of the Zen Sect; but, as I have pointed out in the introduction, the truth of this tradition does not affect the validity of the teaching one way or the other, since Huang Po is surely speaking from a direct experience of the One Mind.

A: Words used to attract the dull of wit are not to be relied on.

Q: If those teachings were meant for the dull-witted, I have yet to hear what Dharma has been taught to those of really high capacity.

A: If they are really men of high capacity, where could they find people to follow? If they seek from within themselves, they will find nothing tangible; how much less can they find a Dharma worthy of their attention elsewhere! Do not look to what is called the Dharma by preachers, for what sort of Dharma could that be?

Q: If that is so, should we not seek for anything at all?

A: By conceding this, you would save yourself a lot of mental effort.

Q: But in this way everything would be eliminated. There cannot just be nothing.

A: Who called it nothing? Who was this fellow? But you wanted to SEEK for something.

Q: Since there is no need to seek, why do you also say that not everything is eliminated?

A: Not to seek is to rest tranquil. Who told you to eliminate anything? Look at the void in front of your eyes. How can you produce it or eliminate it?

Q: If I could reach this Dharma, would it be like the void?

A: Morning and night I have explained to you that the Void is both One and Manifold. I said this as a temporary expedient, but you are building up concepts from it.

Q: Do you mean that we should not form concepts as human beings normally do?

A: I have not prevented you; but concepts are related to the senses; and, when feeling takes place, wisdom is shut out.

53

Q: Then should we avoid any feeling in relation to the Dharma?

A: Where no feeling arises, who can say that you are right?

Q: Why do you speak as though I was mistaken in all the questions I have asked Your Reverence?

A: You are a man who doesn't understand what is said to him. What is all this about being mistaken?[1]

*　　　*　　　*

28. Q: Up to now, you have refuted everything which has been said. You have done nothing to point out the true Dharma to us.

A: In the true Dharma there is no confusion, but you produce confusion by such questions. What sort of 'true Dharma' can you go seeking for?

Q: Since the confusion arises from my questions, what will Your Reverence's answer be?

A: Observe things as they are and don't pay attention to other people. There are some people just like mad dogs barking at everything that moves, even barking when the wind stirs among the grass and leaves.[2]

*　　　*　　　*

29. Regarding this Zen Doctrine of ours, since it was first transmitted, it has never taught that men should seek for learning or form concepts. 'Studying the Way' is just a figure of speech. It is a method of arousing people's interest

[1] Huang Po is obviously trying to help his questioner break away from the habit of thinking in terms of concepts and logical categories. To do this, he is obliged to make his questioner seem wrong, whatever he asks. We are reminded of the Buddha who, when questioned about such things as existence and non-existence, would reply: 'Not this, not this.'

[2] Such people mistake motions taking place within their minds for external independently moving objects.

in the early stages of their development. In fact, the Way is not something which can be studied. Study leads to the retention of concepts and so the Way is entirely misunderstood. Moreover, the Way is not something specially existing; it is called the Mahāyāna Mind—Mind which is not to be found inside, outside or in the middle. Truly it is not located anywhere. The first step is to refrain from knowledge-based concepts. This implies that if you were to follow the empirical method to the utmost limit, on reaching that limit you would still be unable to locate Mind. The way is spiritual Truth and was originally without name or title. It was only because people ignorantly sought for it empirically that the Buddhas appeared and taught them to eradicate this method of approach. Fearing that nobody would understand, they selected the name 'Way'. You must not allow this name to lead you into forming a mental concept of a road. So it is said 'When the fish is caught we pay no more attention to the trap.' When body and mind achieve spontaneity, the Way is reached and Mind is understood. A śramana[1] is so called because he has penetrated to the original source of all things. The fruit of attaining the śramana stage is gained by putting an end to all anxiety; it does not come from book-learning.[2]

[1] Commonly, the word for 'monk'.

[2] This passage has a strong Taoist flavour. The quotation is from Chuang Tzŭ, and the word Tao (Way) is used throughout. Zen and Taoism have so much in common that some have been led to believe that the former is a sort of Taoism in Buddhist disguise; but, as both sects employ much the same theory and practice, it may be that the similarity is because the teachers of both sects are speaking from the same transcendental experience of Reality. The present text is written in a highly condensed form and includes sermons delivered on many different occasions. It is not improbable that paragraphs 29 and 30 are a summary of a sermon delivered to an audience including one or more distinguished Taoist scholars, especially as the opening sentence gives the impression that the Master was addressing newcomers to Zen.

30. If you now set about using your minds to seek Mind, listening to the teaching of others, and hoping to reach the goal through mere learning, when will you ever succeed? Some of the ancients had sharp minds; they no sooner heard the Doctrine proclaimed than they hastened to discard all learning. So they were called 'Sages who, abandoning learning, have come to rest in spontaneity'.[1] In these days people only seek to stuff themselves with knowledge and deductions, seeking everywhere for book-knowledge and calling this 'Dharma-practice'.[2] They do not know that so much knowledge and deduction have just the contrary effect of piling up obstacles. Merely acquiring a lot of knowledge makes you like a child who gives himself indigestion by gobbling too much curds. Those who study the Way according to the Three Vehicles are all like this. All you can call them is people who suffer from indigestion. When so-called knowledge and deductions are not digested, they become poisons, for they belong only to the plane of samsāra. In the Absolute, there is nothing at all of this kind. So it is said: 'In the armoury of my sovereign, there is no Sword of Thusness'. All the concepts you have formed in the past must be discarded and replaced by void. Where dualism ceases, there is the Void of the Womb of Tathāgatas. The term 'Womb of Tathāgatas' implies that not the smallest hairsbreadth of anything can exist there. That is why the Dharma Rāja (*the Buddha*), who broke down the notion of objective existence, manifested himself in this

---

[1] This passage contains another famous Taoist term—WU WEI, sometimes mistranslated 'non-action'. In fact, it means no calculated action, nothing but spontaneous actions required to meet the demands of the passing moment.

[2] Literacy is by no means essential to the mastery of Zen. The *Tibetan Book of the Great Liberation* makes the same point.

world, and that is why he said: 'When I was with Dīpaṃ-kara Buddha there was not a particle of anything for me to attain.' This saying is intended just to void your sense-based knowledge and deductions. Only he who restrains every vestige of empiricism and ceases to rely upon anything can become a perfectly tranquil man. The canonical teachings of the Three Vehicles are just remedies for temporary needs. They were taught to meet such needs and so are of temporary value and differ one from another. If only this could be understood, there would be no more doubts about it. Above all it is essential not to select some particular teaching suited to a certain occasion, and, being impressed by its forming part of the written canon, regard it as an immutable concept. Why so? Because in truth there is no unalterable Dharma which the Tathāgata could have preached. People of our sect would never argue that there could be such a thing. We just know how to put all mental activity to rest and thus achieve tranquillity. We certainly do not begin by thinking things out and end up in perplexity.

*   *   *

31. Q: From all you have just said, Mind is the Buddha; but it is not clear as to what sort of mind is meant by this 'Mind which is the Buddha'.

A: How many minds have you got?

Q: But is the Buddha the ordinary mind or the Enlightened mind?

A: Where on earth do you keep your 'ordinary mind' and your 'Enlightened mind'?

Q: In the teaching of the Three Vehicles it is stated that there are both. Why does Your Reverence deny it?

A: In the teaching of the Three Vehicles it is clearly explained that the ordinary and Enlightened minds are illusions. You don't understand. All this clinging to the idea of things existing is to mistake vacuity for the truth. How can such conceptions not be illusory? Being illusory, they hide Mind from you. If you would only rid yourselves of the concepts of ordinary and Enlightened, you would find that there is no other Buddha than the Buddha in your own Mind. When Bodhidharma came from the West, he just pointed out that the substance of which all men are composed is the Buddha. You people go on misunderstanding; you hold to concepts such as 'ordinary' and 'Enlightened', directing your thoughts outwards where they gallop about like horses! All this amounts to beclouding your own minds! So I tell you Mind is the Buddha. As soon as thought or sensation arises, you fall into dualism. Beginningless time and the present moment are the same. There is no this and no that. To understand this truth is called compete and unexcelled Enlightenment.

Q: Upon what Doctrine (*Dharma-principles*) does Your Reverence base these words?

A: Why seek a doctrine? As soon as you have a doctrine, you fall into dualistic thought.

Q: Just now you said that the beginningless past and the present are the same. What do you mean by that?

A: It is just because of your SEEKING that you make a difference between them. If you were to stop seeking, how could there be any difference between them?

Q: If they are not different, why did you employ separate terms for them?

A: If you hadn't mentioned ordinary and Enlightened, who would have bothered to say such things? Just as those categories have no real existence, so Mind is not really 'mind'. And, as both Mind and those categories are really illusions, wherever can you hope to find anything?

*   *   *

32. Q: Illusion can hide from us our own mind, but up to now you have not taught us how to get rid of illusion.

A: The arising and the elimination of illusion are both illusory. Illusion is not something rooted in Reality; it exists because of your dualistic thinking. If you will only cease to indulge in opposed concepts such as 'ordinary' and 'Enlightened', illusion will cease of itself. And then if you still want to destroy it wherever it may be, you will find that there is not a hairsbreadth left of anything on which to lay hold. This is the meaning of: 'I will let go with both hands, for then I shall certainly discover the Buddha in my Mind.'

Q: If there is nothing on which to lay hold, how is the Dharma to be transmitted?

A: It is a transmission of Mind with Mind.

Q: If Mind is used for transmission, why do you say that Mind too does not exist?

A: Obtaining no Dharma whatever is called Mind transmission. The understanding of this Mind implies no Mind and no Dharma.

Q: If there is no Mind and no Dharma, what is meant by transmission?

A: You hear people speak of Mind transmission and then you talk of something to be received. So Bodhidharma said:

The nature of the Mind when understood,
No human speech can compass or disclose.
Enlightenment is naught to be attained,
And he that gains it does not say he knows.

If I were to make this clear to you, I doubt if you could stand up to it.

*　　　　*　　　　*

33. Q: Surely the void stretching out in front of our eyes is objective. Then aren't you pointing to something objective and seeing Mind in it?

A: What sort of mind could I tell you to see in an objective environment? Even if you could see it, it would only be Mind reflected in an objective sphere. You would be like a man looking at his face in a mirror; though you could distinguish your features in it clearly, you would still be looking at a mere reflection. What bearing has this on the affair that brought you to me?

Q: If we do not see by means of reflections, when shall we see at all?

A: So long as you are concerned with 'by means of', you will always be depending on something false. When will you ever succeed in understanding? Instead of observing those who tell you to open wide both your hands like one who has nothing to lose, you waste your strength bragging about all sorts of things.

Q: To those who understand, even reflections are nothing?

A: If solid things do not exist, how much the less can we make use of reflections. Don't go about babbling like a dreamer with his eyes open (*like a sleepwalker*).

Stepping into the public hall, His Reverence said: Having many sorts of knowledge cannot compare with giving up SEEKING for anything, which is the best of all things. Mind is not of several kinds and there is no Doctrine which can be put into words. As there is no more to be said, the assembly is dismissed!

*   *   *

34. Q: What is meant by relative truth?[1]

A: What would you do with such a parasitical plant as that? Reality is perfect purity; why base a discussion on false terms? To be absolutely without concepts is called the Wisdom of Dispassion. Every day, whether walking, standing, sitting or lying down, and in all your speech, remain detached from everything within the sphere of phenomena. Whether you speak or merely blink an eye, let it be done with complete dispassion. Now we are getting towards the end of the third period of five hundred years since the time of the Buddha, and most students of Zen cling to all sorts of sounds and forms. Why do they not copy me by letting each thought go as though it were nothing, or as though it were a piece of rotten wood, a stone, or the cold ashes of a dead fire? Or else, by just making whatever slight response is suited to each occasion? If you do not act thus, when you reach the end of your days here, you will be tortured by Yama.[2] You must get away from the doctrines of existence and non-existence, for Mind is like the sun, forever in the void, shining spontaneously, shining without

---

[1] Literally 'worldly truth' no doubt used in the sense of 'truths' applicable to the apparently objective sphere of daily life.
[2] The King of Hell—here used figuratively.

intending to shine. This is not something which you can accomplish without effort, but when you reach the point of clinging to nothing whatever, you will be acting as the Buddhas act. This will indeed be acting in accordance with the saying: 'Develop a mind which rests on no thing whatever.[1] For this is your pure Dharmakāya, which is called supreme perfect Enlightenment. If you cannot understand this, though you gain profound knowledge from your studies, though you make the most painful efforts and practise the most stringent austerities, you will still fail to know your own mind. All your effort will have been misdirected and you will certainly join the family of Māra.[2] What advantage can you gain from this sort of practice? As Chih Kung[3] once said: 'The Buddha is really the creation of your own Mind. How, then, can he be sought through scriptures?' Though you study how to attain the Three Grades of Bodhisattvahood, the Four Grades of Sainthood, and the Ten Stages of a Bodhisattva's Progress to Enlightenment until your mind is full of them, you will merely be balancing yourself between 'ordinary' and 'Enlightened'. Not to see that all METHODS of following the Way are ephemeral is samsāric Dharma.

> Its strength once spent, the arrow falls to earth.
> You build up lives which won't fulfil your hopes.
> How far below the Transcendental Gate
> From which one leap will gain the Buddha's realm![4]

[1] A famous quotation from the Diamond Sūtra.
[2] Prince of Devils—here used figuratively.
[3] A famous sixth-century monk.
[4] This verse is from the 'Song of Enlightenment' attributed to Yung Chia, a seven-century monk. This fascinating work has been translated in full by Dr. Walter Liebenthal and published in the *Journal of Oriental Studies of the Catholic University of Peiping*, Vol. VI, 1941.

It is because you are not that sort of man that you insist on a thorough study of the methods established by people of old for gaining knowledge on the conceptual level. Chih Kung also said: 'If you do not meet a transcendental teacher, you will have swallowed the Mahāyāna medicine in vain!'

*   *   *

35. If you would spend all your time—walking, standing, sitting or lying down—learning to halt the concept-forming activities of your own mind, you could be sure of ultimately attaining the goal. Since your strength is insufficient, you might not be able to transcend saṁsāra by a single leap; but, after five or ten years, you would surely have made a good beginning and be able to make further progress spontaneously. It is because you are not that sort of man that you feel obliged to employ your mind 'studying dhyāna' and 'studying the Way'. What has all that got to do with Buddhism? So it is said that all the Tathāgata taught was just to convert people; it was like pretending yellow leaves are real gold just to stop the flow of a child's tears; it must by no means be regarded as though it were ultimate truth. If you take it for truth, you are no member of our sect; and what bearing can it have on your original substance? So the sūtra says: 'What is called supreme perfect wisdom implies that there is really nothing whatever to be attained.' If you are also able to understand this, you will realize that the Way of the Buddhas and the Way of devils are equally wide of the mark. The original pure, glistening universe is neither square nor round, big nor small; it is without any such distinctions as long and short,

it is beyond attachment and activity, ignorance and Enlightenment. You must see clearly that there is really nothing at all—no humans and no Buddhas. The great chiliocosms, numberless as grains of sand, are mere bubbles. All wisdom and all holiness are but streaks of lightning. None of them have the reality of Mind. The Dharmakāya, from ancient times until today, together with the Buddhas and Patriarchs, is One. How can it lack a single hair of anything? Even if you understand this, you must make the most strenuous efforts. Throughout this life, you can never be certain of living long enough to take another breath.[1]

*   *   *

36. Q: The Sixth Patriarch was illiterate. How is it that he was handed the robe which elevated him to that office? Elder Shên Hsiu (*a rival candidate*) occupied a position above five hundred others and, as a teaching monk, he was able to expound thirty-two volumes of sūtras. Why did he not receive the robe?

A: Because he still indulged in conceptual thought—in a dharma of activity. To him 'as you practise, so shall you attain' was a reality. So the Fifth Patriarch made the transmission to Hui Nêng (*Wei Lang*). At that very moment, the latter attained a tacit understanding and received in silence the profoundest thought of the Tathāgata. That is why the Dharma was transmitted to him. You do not see that THE FUNDAMENTAL DOCTRINE OF THE DHARMA IS THAT THERE ARE NO DHARMAS, YET THAT THIS DOCTRINE OF NO-DHARMA

---

[1] Buddhists believe that it is a rare and difficult thing to be born a human being; and, as Enlightenment can only be attained from the human state, it is a matter of great urgency that we should press forward. Otherwise, the unique opportunity may be lost for many aeons.

IS IN ITSELF A DHARMA; AND NOW THAT THE NO-DHARMA
DOCTRINE HAS BEEN TRANSMITTED, HOW CAN THE DOCTRINE
OF THE DHARMA BE A DHARMA?[1] Whoever understands the
meaning of this deserves to be called a monk, one skilled
at 'Dharma-practice'. If you do not believe this, you must
explain the following story. 'The Elder Wei Ming climbed
to the summit of the Ta Yü Mountain to visit the Sixth
Patriarch. The latter asked him why he had come. Was it
for the robe or for the Dharma? The Elder Wei Ming
answered that he had not come for the robe, but only for
the Dharma; whereupon the Sixth Patriarch said: "Perhaps
you will concentrate your thoughts for a moment and avoid
thinking in terms of good and evil." Ming did as he was
told, and the Sixth Patriarch continued: "While you are
not thinking of good and not thinking of evil, just at this
very moment, return to what you were before your father
and mother were born." Even as the words were spoken,
Ming arrived at a sudden tacit understanding. Accordingly
he bowed to the ground and said: "I am like a man drinking water who knows in himself how cool it is. I have lived
with the Fifth Patriarch and his disciples for thirty years,
but it is only today that I am able to banish the mistakes
in my former way of thinking." The Sixth Patriarch replied: "Just so. Now at last you understand why, when the

[1] This passage has puzzled many a Chinese scholar. I am not sure
that this translation conveys the meaning very well, but at least I have
simplified the wording by using 'doctrine' as well as 'dharma'. In the
original, the same word is used for both. A word-for-word translation
would run something like this: 'Dharma original Dharma not Dharma,
not Dharma Dharma also Dharma, now transmit not Dharma Dharma,
Dharma Dharma how-can be Dharma.' I have closely followed a
rendering made for me some years ago by Mr. I. T. Pun, a famous
Buddhist scholar resident in Hongkong. He admits that this version
merely represents his own opinion, but it seems to me the best possible.
In my previous published translation I failed lamentably.

First Patriarch arrived from India, he just pointed directly at men's Minds, by which they could perceive their real Nature and become Buddhas, and why he never spoke of anything besides." ' Have we not seen how, when Ānanda asked Kāśyapa what the World Honoured had transmitted to him in addition to the golden robe, the latter exclaimed, 'Ānanda!' and, upon Ānanda's respectfully answering 'Yes?', continued: 'Throw down the flagpole at the monastery gate.' Such was the sign which the First (*Indian*) Patriarch gave him. For thirty years the wise Ānanda ministered to the Buddha's personal needs; but, because he was too fond of acquiring knowledge, the Buddha admonished him, saying: 'If you pursue knowledge for a thousand days, that will avail you less than one day's proper study of the Way. If you do not study it, you will be unable to digest even a single drop of water!'

PART TWO

THE WAN LING RECORD OF THE
ZEN MASTER HUANG PO (TUAN CHI)

A collection of dialogues, sermons and anecdotes recorded by P'ei Hsiu during his tenure of the prefecture of Wan Ling

1. Once I put this question to the Master. How many of the four or five hundred persons gathered here on this mountain have fully understood Your Reverence's teaching?

The Master answered: Their number cannot be known. Why? Because my Way is through Mind-awakening. How can it be conveyed in words? Speech only produces some effect when it falls on the uninstructed ears of children.

*　　　*　　　*

2. Q: What is the Buddha?[1]

A: Mind is the Buddha, while the cessation of conceptual thought is the Way. Once you stop arousing concepts and thinking in terms of existence and non-existence, long and short, other and self, active and passive, and suchlike, you will find that your Mind is intrinsically the Buddha, that the Buddha is intrinsically Mind, and that Mind resembles a void.[2] Therefore is it written that 'the true Dharmakāya[3]

---

[1] The Absolute.
[2] Meaning intangible, not a mere negation.
[3] The Absolute Body of a Buddha.

67

resembles a void'. Seek for naught besides this, else your search must end in sorrow. Though you perform the six pāramitās[1] for as many aeons as there are grains of sand in the Ganges, adding also all the other sorts of activities for gaining Enlightenment, YOU WILL STILL FALL SHORT OF THE GOAL. Why? Because these are karma-forming activities and, when the good karma they produce has been exhausted, you will be born again in the ephemeral world. Therefore is it also written: 'The Samboghkāya[2] is not a real Buddha, nor a real teacher of the Dharma.[3] Only come to know the nature of your own Mind, in which there is no self and no other, and you will in fact be a Buddha!

*   *   *

3. Q: Allowing that the Enlightened man who achieves the cessation of conceptual thought is Buddha, would not an ignorant man, on ceasing to think conceptually, lose himself in oblivion?

A: There ARE no Enlightened men or ignorant men, and there IS no oblivion. Yet, though basically everything is without objective existence, you must not come to think in terms of anything non-existent; and though things are not non-existent, you must not form a concept of anything existing. For 'existence' and 'non-existence' are both empirical concepts no better than illusions. Therefore it is written: 'Whatever the senses apprehend resembles an

---

[1] Charity, morality, patience under affliction, zealous application, right control of the mind, and the application of highest wisdom.

[2] Buddha's Body of Bliss.

[3] This means that the idealized or heavenly form of a Buddha, to whom the Unenlightened pray, is unreal in that he is regarded as an entity and therefore as apart from the One Mind.

illusion, including everything ranging from mental concepts to living beings.' Our Founder[1] preached to his disciples naught but total abstraction leading to elimination of sense-perception. In this total abstraction does the Way of the Buddhas flourish; while from discrimination between this and that a host of demons blazes forth!

* * *

4. Q: If Mind and the Buddha[2] are intrinsically one, should we continue to practise the six pāramitās and the other orthodox means of gaining Enlightenment?

A: Enlightenment springs from Mind, regardless of your practice of the six pāramitās and the rest. All such practices are merely expedients for handling 'concrete' matters when dealing with the problems of daily life. Even Enlightenment, the Absolute, Reality, Sudden Attainment, the Dharmakāya and all the others down to the Ten Stages of Progress, the Four Rewards of virtuous and wise living and the State of Holiness and Wisdom are—every one of them —mere concepts for helping us through saṁsāra; they have nothing to do with the real Buddha-Mind. Since Mind is the Buddha, the ideal way of attainment is to cultivate that Buddha-Mind. Only avoid conceptual thoughts, which lead to becoming and cessation, to the afflictions of the sentient world and all the rest; then you will have no need of methods of Enlightenment and suchlike. Therefore is it written:

> All the Buddha's teachings just had this single object—
> To carry us beyond the stage of thought.
> Now, if I accomplish cessation of my thinking,
> What use to me the Dharmas Buddha taught?

[1] Bodhidarma.
[2] Absolute.

69

From Gautama Buddha down through the whole line
of patriarchs to Bodhidharma, none preached aught besides
the One Mind, otherwise known as the Sole Vehicle of
Liberation. Hence, though you search throughout the whole
universe, you will never find another vehicle. Nowhere has
this teaching leaves or branches; its one quality is eternal
truth. Hence it is a teaching hard to accept. When Bodhidharma came to China and reached the Kingdoms of Liang
and Wei, only the Venerable Master Ko gained a silent
insight into our own Mind; as soon as it was explained to
him, he understood that Mind is the Buddha, and that
individual mind and body are nothing. This teaching is
called the Great Way. The very nature of the Great Way
is voidness of opposition. Bodhidharma firmly believed in
being ONE WITH THE REAL 'SUBSTANCE' OF THE UNIVERSE IN
THIS LIFE! Mind and that 'substance' do not differ one jot—
that 'substance' IS Mind. They cannot possibly be separated.
It was for this revelation that he earned the title of Patriarch
of our sect, and therefore is it written: 'The moment of
realizing the unity of Mind and the "substance" which
constitutes reality may truly be said to baffle description.'

*   *   *

5. Q: Does the Buddha really liberate sentient beings?[1]
   A: There are in reality no sentient beings to be delivered
by the Tathāgata. If even self has no objective existence,
how much less has other-than-self! Thus, neither Buddha
nor sentient beings exist objectively.

*   *   *

[1] From saṁsāra—the endless round of birth and death.

6. Q: Yet it is recorded that 'Whosoever possesses the thirty-two characteristic signs of a Buddha is able to deliver sentient beings'. How can you deny it?

A: Anything possessing ANY signs is illusory. It is by perceiving that all signs are no signs that you perceive the Tathāgata.[1] 'Buddha' and 'sentient beings' are both your own false conceptions. It is because you do not know real Mind that you delude yourselves with such objective concepts. If you WILL conceive of a Buddha, YOU WILL BE OBSTRUCTED BY THAT BUDDHA!!! And when you conceive of sentient beings, you will be obstructed by those beings. All such dualistic concepts as 'ignorant' and 'Enlightened', 'pure' and 'impure', are obstructions. It is because your minds are hindered by them that the Wheel of the Law must be turned.[2] Just as apes spend their time throwing things away and picking them up again unceasingly, so it is with you and your learning. All you need is to give up your 'learning', your 'ignorant' and 'Enlightened', 'pure' and 'impure', 'great' and 'little', your 'attachment' and 'activity'. Such things are mere conveniences, mere ornaments within the One Mind. I hear you have studied the sūtras of the twelve divisions of the Three Vehicles. They are all mere empirical concepts. Really you must give them up!

So just discard all you have acquired as being no better than a bed spread for you when you were sick. Only when you have abandoned all perceptions, there being nothing objective to perceive; only when phenomena obstruct you no longer; only when you have rid yourself of the whole gamut of dualistic concepts of the 'ignorant' and 'En-

[1] Buddha.
[2] I.e. that the relative truths of orthodox Buddhism must be taught.

lightened' category, will you at last earn the title of Transcendental Buddha. Therefore is it written: 'Your prostrations are in vain. Put no faith in such ceremonies. Hie
from such false beliefs.' Since Mind knows no divisions into
separate entities, phenomena must be equally undifferentiated. Since Mind is above all activities, so must it be with
phenomena. Every phenomenon that exists is a creation of
thought; therefore I need but empty my mind to discover
that all of them are void. It is the same with all sense-
objects, to whichever of the myriads of categories they
belong. The entire void stretching out in all directions is
of one substance with Mind; and, since Mind is fundamentally undifferentiated, so must it be with everything
else. Different entities appear to you only because your
perceptions differ—just as the colours of the precious
delicacies eaten by the Devas are said to differ in accordance with the individual merits of the Devas eating
them!

Anuttara–samyak–sambodhi[1] is a name for the realization that the Buddhas of the whole universe do not in fact
possess the smallest perceptible attribute. There exists just
the One Mind. Truly there are no multiplicity of forms, no
Celestial Brilliance, and no Glorious Victory (*over samsāra*)
or submission to the Victor.[2] Since no Glorious Victory was
ever won, there can be no such formal entity as a Buddha;
and, since no submission ever took place, there can be no
such formal entities as sentient beings.

*   *   *

7. Q: Even though Mind be formless, how can you deny

[1] Supreme Omniscience.
[2] Buddha.

the existence of the Thirty-Two Characteristic Signs of a Buddha, or of the Eighty Excellencies whereby people have been ferried over?[1]

A: The Thirty-Two Signs are signs,[2] and whatever has form is illusory. The Eighty Excellencies belong to the sphere of matter; but whoever perceives a self in matter is travelling the wrong path; he cannot comprehend the Tathāgata thus.

*   *   *

8. Q: Does the essential substance of the Buddha differ at all from that of sentient beings or are they identical?

A: Essential substance partakes neither of identity nor difference. If you accept the orthodox teachings of the Three Vehicles of Buddhism, discriminating between the Buddha-Nature and the nature of sentient beings, you will create for yourself Three Vehicle karma, and identities and differences will result. But if you accept the Buddha-Vehicle, which is the doctrine transmitted by Bodhidharma, you will not speak of such things; you will merely point to the One Mind which is without identity or difference, without cause or effect.[3] Therefore is it written: 'There is only the way of the One Vehicle; there is neither a second nor a third, except for those ways employed by the Buddha as purely relative expedients (*upāya*) for the liberation of beings lost in delusion.'

*   *   *

[1] From saṁsāra to Nirvāna.
[2] I.e. forms.
[3] It is not Huang Po's intention to deny the validity of karmic law as it applies to the ephemeral world of saṁsāra.

9. Q: Why was the Bodhisattva of Infinite Extent unable to view the sacred sign on the crown of the Buddha's head?[1]

A: There was really nothing for him to see. Why? The Bodhisattva of Infinite Extent WAS the Tathāgata; it follows that the need to look did not arise. The parable is intended to prevent your conceiving of the Buddha and of sentient beings as entities and thereby falling into the error of spacial separateness. It is a warning against conceiving of entities as existing or not existing and thereby falling into the error of special separateness, and against conceiving of individuals as ignorant or Enlightened and thereby falling into that same error. Only one entirely liberated from concepts can possess a body of infinite extent. All conceptual thinking is called erroneous belief. The upholders of such false doctrines delight in a multiplicity of concepts, but the Bodhisattva remains unmoved amid a whole host of them. 'Tathāgata' means the THUSNESS of all phenomena. Therefore it is written: 'Maitreya is THUS; saints and sages are THUS.' THUSNESS consists in not being subject to becoming or to destruction; THUSNESS consists in not being seen and in not being heard. The crown of the Tathāgata's head is a concept of perfection, but it is also no-perfection-to-be-conceived. So do not fall into conceiving of perfection objectively. It follows that the Buddhakāya[2] is above all activity:[3] therefore must you beware of discriminating between the myriads of separate forms.

The ephemeral may be likened to mere emptiness;[4] the

---

[1] It is clear that this question was asked by somebody not present during the previous discussions.
[2] Absolute.
[3] I.e. activity in production of form.
[4] Flux.

Great Void is perfection wherein is neither lack nor super-fluity, a uniform quiescence in which all activity is stilled.[1] Do not argue that there may be other regions lying outside the Great Void, for such an argument would inevitably lead to discrimination. Therefore is it written: 'Perfection[2] is a deep sea of wisdom; saṃsāra[3] is like a whirling chaos.'

When we talk of the knowledge 'I' may gain, the learn-ing 'I' may achieve, 'my' intuitive understanding, 'my' deliverence from rebirth, and 'my' moral way of living, our successes make these concepts seem pleasant to us, but our failures make them appear deplorable. What is the use of all that? I advise you to remain uniformly quiescent and above all activity. Do not deceive yourselves with concep-tual thinking, and do not look anywhere for the truth, for all that is needed is to refrain from allowing concepts to arise. It is obvious that mental concepts and external per-ceptions are equally misleading, and that the Way of the Buddhas[4] is as dangerous to you as the way of demons. Thus, when Mañjuśrī temporarily entered into dualism, he found himself dwarfed by two iron mountains which made egress impossible. But Mañjuśrī[5] had true under-standing, while Samantabhadra[6] possessed only ephemeral knowledge. Nevertheless, when true understanding and

---

[1] A distinction is here made between 'void' in the sense of flux where all forms are seen in dissolution, and the Great Void which overspreads, penetrates and is all. When the scientists speak of the stuff of the world as mind-stuff, it is probable that they are speaking of the flux, for the Great Void can hardly have been deduced from laws governing the ephemeral world of transitory phenomena. Compared with the Great Void, 'mind-stuff' is a relatively substantial concept!

[2] Nirvāṇa.
[3] The transient universe.
[4] If conceived objectively.
[5] The personification of Ultimate Wisdom.
[6] The personification of Love and Action.

ephemeral knowledge are properly integrated, it will be found that they no longer exist. There is only the One Mind, Mind which is neither Buddha nor sentient beings, for it contains no such dualism. As soon as you conceive of the Buddha, you are forced to conceive of sentient beings, or of concepts and no-concepts, of vital and trivial ones, which will surely imprison you between those two iron mountains.

On account of the obstacles created by dualistic reasoning, Bodhidharma merely pointed to the original Mind and substance of us all as being in fact the Buddha. He offered no false means of self-perfecting oneself; he belonged to no school of gradual attainment. His doctrine admits of no such attributes as light and dark. Since it[1] is not light, lo there is no light; since it is not dark, lo there is no dark! Hence it follows that there is no Darkness,[2] nor End of Darkness.[3] Whosoever enters the gateway of our sect must deal with everything solely by means of the intellect.[4] This sort of perception is known as the Dharma; as the Dharma is perceived, we speak of Buddha; while perceiving that in fact there are no Dharma and no Buddha is called entering the Saṇgha, who are otherwise known as 'monks dwelling above all activity'; and the whole sequence may be called the Triratna or Three Jewels in one Substance.[5]

[1] Truth.
[2] Avidyā or primordial ignorance.
[3] Enlightenment.
[4] Here, 'intellect' stands for MANAS, the highest faculty of the human mind by which a man rises from conceptual thought to intuitive knowledge.
[5] Huang Po is juggling with the most sacred of Buddhist terms, perhaps causing some of his hearers to stiffen with disapproval, but clearly in the hope of shocking them into a deeper understanding of truth. The terse humour with which he cloaks his underlying sincerity is lost in the translation.

76

Those who seek the Dharma[1] must not seek from the Buddha, nor from the Dharma[2] nor from the Saṇgha. They should seek from nowhere. When the Buddha is not sought, there IS no Buddha to be found! When the Dharma is not sought, there IS no Dharma to be found! When the Saṇgha is not sought, there IS no Saṇgha!

*   *   *

10. Q: You yourself are a member of the Saṇgha now, obviously engaged in preaching the Dharma. Then how can you declare that neither of them exists?

A: If you suppose there is a Dharma to be preached, you will naturally ask me to expound it, but if you postulate a 'ME', that implies a spacial entity! The Dharma is NO Dharma—it is MIND! Therefore Bodhidharma said:

> Though I handed down Mind's Dharma,
> How can Dharma be a Dharma?
> For neither Mind nor Dharma
> Can objectively exist.
> Only thus you'll understand
> The Dharma that is passed with Mind to Mind.

Knowing that in truth not a single thing exists which can be attained![3] is called sitting in a bodhimandala.[4] A bodhimandala is a state in which no concepts arise, in which you awaken to the intrinsic voidness of phenomena, also called the utter voidness of the Womb of Tathāgatas.[5]

---

[1] Truth.
[2] Doctrine.
[3] Grasped, perceived, conceived, etc.
[4] A sanctuary for attaining Enlightenment.
[5] The source of all phenomena.

There's never been a single thing;
Then where's defiling dust to cling?
If you can reach the heart of this,
Why talk of transcendental bliss?[1]

*   *   *

11. Q: If 'there's never been a single thing', can we speak of phenomena as non-existent?

A: 'Non-existent' is just as wrong as its opposite. Bodhi means having no concept of existence or non-existence.

*   *   *

12. Q: What is the Buddha?[2]

A: Your Mind is the Buddha. The Buddha is Mind. Mind and Buddha are indivisible. Therefore it is written: 'That which is Mind is the Buddha; if it is other than Mind, it is certainly other than Buddha.'

*   *   *

13. Q: If our own Mind is the Buddha, how did Bodhidharma transmit his doctrine when he came from India?

A: When he came from India, he transmitted only Mind-Buddha. He just pointed to the truth that the minds

---

[1] This famous poem of Hui Nêng is intended to refute the view that Mind is a mirror to be cleansed of the defiling dust of phenomena, passion and other illusions, for this view leads to dualism, besides implying a certain degree of objectivity in the nature of mind. The dust and the mirror are one intangible unity.

[2] The questioner seems to be a newcomer.

of all of you have from the very first been identical with the Buddha, and in no way separate from each other. That is why we call him our Patriarch. Whoever has an instant understanding of this truth suddenly transcends the whole hierarchy of saints and adepts belonging to any of the Three Vehicles. You have always been one with the Buddha, so do not pretend you can ATTAIN to this oneness by various practices.[1]

14. Q: If that is so, what Dharma do all the Buddhas teach when they manifest themselves in the world?

A: When all the Buddhas manifest themselves in the world, they proclaim nothing but the One Mind. Thus, Gautama Buddha silently transmitted to Mahākāśyapa the doctrine that the One Mind, which is the substance of all things, is co-extensive with the Void and fills the entire world of phenomena. This is called the Law of All the Buddhas. Discuss it as you may, how can you even hope to approach the truth through words? Nor can it be perceived either subjectively or objectively. So full understanding can come to you only through an inexpressible mystery. The approach to it is called the Gateway of the Stillness beyond all Activity. If you wish to understand, know that a sudden comprehension comes when the mind has been purged of all the clutter of conceptual and discriminatory thought-activity. Those who seek the truth by means of intellect and learning only get further and further away from it. Not till your thoughts cease all their branching here and there, not till you abandon all thoughts of seeking for something, not till your

---

[1] We cannot BECOME what we have always been; we can only become intuitively aware of our original state, previously hidden from us by the clouds of māyā.

mind is motionless as wood or stone, will you be on the right road to the Gate.[1]

*　　　　*　　　　*

15. Q: At this very moment, all sorts of erroneous thoughts are constantly flowing through our minds. How can you speak of our having none?

A: Error has no substance; it is entirely the product of your own thinking. If you know that Mind is the Buddha and that Mind is fundamentally without error, whenever thoughts arise, you will be fully convinced that THEY are responsible for errors. If you could prevent all conceptual movements of thought and still your thinking-processes, naturally there would be no error left in you. Therefore is it said: 'When thoughts arise, then do all things arise. When thoughts vanish, then do all things vanish.'

*　　　　*　　　　*

16. Q: At this moment, while erroneous thoughts are arising in my mind, where is the Buddha?[2]

A: At this moment you are conscious of those erroneous

---

[1] These words recall the admonitions of so many mystics—Buddhist, Christian, Hindu or Sufi—who have committed their experience to words. What Huang Po calls the total abandonment of HSIN—mind, thought, perceptions, concepts and the rest—implies the utter surrender of self insisted on by Sufi and Christian mystics. Indeed, in paragraph 28 he used the very words: 'LET THE SELF PERISH UTTERLY'. Such striking unanimity of expression by mystics widely separated in time and space can hardly be attributed to coincidence. No several persons entirely unacquainted with one another could produce such closely similar accounts of purely imaginary journeys. Hence one is led to suppose that what they describe is real. This seems to have been Aldous Huxley's view when he compiled that valuable work *The Perennial Philosophy*.

[2] Is the One Mind then no longer present in me?

80

thoughts. Well, your consciousness is the Buddha! Perhaps you can understand that, were you but free of these delusory mental processes, there would then be no 'Buddha'. Why so? Because when you allow a movement of your mind to result in a concept of the Buddha, you are bringing into existence an objective being capable of being Enlightened. Similarly, any concept of sentient beings in need of deliverance CREATES such beings as objects of your thoughts. All intellectual processes and movements of thought result from your concepts.[1] If you were to refrain from conceptualizing altogether, where could the Buddha continue to exist? You are in the same predicament as Mañjuśrī who, as soon as he permitted himself to conceive of the Buddha as an objective entity, was dwarfed and hemmed in on all sides by those two iron mountains.

*   *   *

17. Q: At the moment of Enlightenment, where is the Buddha?

A: Whence does your question proceed? Whence does your consciousness arise? When speech is silenced, all movement stilled, every sight and sound vanished—THEN is the Buddha's work of deliverence truly going forward! Then, where will you seek the Buddha? You cannot place a head upon your head, or lips upon your lips; rather, you should just refrain from every kind of dualistic distinction.[2] Hills are hills. Water is water. Monks are monks. Laymen are laymen. But these mountains, these rivers, the whole world

---

[1] Which bring the corresponding thought objects into existence.
[2] Since we are the Buddha, to seek him elsewhere is to place a head upon our head.

itself, together with sun, moon and stars—not one of them exists outside your minds! The vast chiliocosm exists only within you, so where else can the various categories of phenomena possibly be found? Outside Mind, there is nothing. The green hills which everywhere meet your gaze and that void sky that you see glistening above the earth— not a hairsbreadth of any of them exists outside the concepts you have formed for yourself! So it is that every single sight and sound is but the Buddha's Eye of Wisdom.[1]

Phenomena do not arise independently but rely upon environment.[2] And it is their appearing as objects which necessitates all sorts of individualized knowledge. You may talk the whole day through, yet what has been said? You may listen from dawn till dusk, yet what will you have heard? Thus, though Gautama Buddha preached for forty-nine years, in truth no word was spoken.[3]

*　　　*　　　*

18. Q: Assuming all this is so, what particular state is connoted by the word Bodhi?[4]

A: Bodhi is no state. The Buddha did not attain to it. Sentient beings do not lack it. It cannot be reached with the body nor sought with the mind. All sentient beings ARE ALREADY of one form with Bodhi.

[1] The Buddha's Eye of Wisdom commonly means the eye with which he perceives the true unity of all things. Huang Po, however, does not say 'perceived BY the Eye', but uses the phrase 'IS the Eye', thereby identifying see-er and seen.

[2] I.e. the mental environment created by us.

[3] Words belong to the realm of flux and illusion. The truth is beyond words, a silent and profound experience. The Buddha spoke of relative means. Viewed absolutely, no word was spoken.

[4] Enlightenment or Supreme Wisdom.

19. Q: But how does one 'Attain to the Bodhi-Mind'?

A: Bodhi is not something to be attained.[1] If, at this very moment, you could convince yourselves of its unattainability, being certain indeed that nothing at all can ever be attained, you would already be Bodhi-minded. Since Bodhi is not a state, it is nothing for you to attain. And therefore is it written of Gautama Buddha: 'While I was yet in the realm of Dīpaṃkara Buddha, there was not a grain of anything to be attained by me. It was then that Dīpaṃkara Buddha made his prophecy that I, too, should become a Buddha.' If you know positively that all sentient beings are already one with Bodhi, you will cease thinking of Bodhi as something to be attained. You may recently have heard others talking about this 'attaining of the Bodhi-Mind', but this may be called an intellectual way of driving the Buddha away! By following this method, you only APPEAR to achieve Buddhahood; if you were to spend aeon upon aeon in that way, you would only achieve the Sambhogakāya and Nirmāṇakāya. What connection would all that have with your original and real Buddha-Nature?[2] Therefore is it written: 'Seeking outside for a Buddha possessed of form has nothing to do with you.'

*   *   *

20. Q: If we have always been one with the Buddha (*Absolute*), why are there nevertheless beings who come into

[1] Perceived, grasped, entered, realized, conceived, etc.

[2] I.e. you would achieve the physical and spiritual aspects of a Buddha, which an Enlightened One bears within the various realms of transitory existence, but you would lack the Dharmakāya, the aspect of a Buddha as identical with the Absolute.

existence through the four kinds of birth and enter the six states of existence, each with the characteristic form and appearance of its kind?

A: The essential Buddha-Substance is a perfect whole, without superfluity or lack. It permeates the six states of existence and yet is everywhere perfectly whole. Thus, every single one of the myriads of phenomena in the universe IS the Buddha (*Absolute*). This substance may be likened to a quantity of quicksilver which, being scattered in all directions, everywhere re-forms into perfect wholes. When undispersed, it is of one piece, the one comprising the whole and the whole comprising the one. The various forms and appearances, on the other hand, may be likened to dwellings. Just as one abandons a stable in favour of a house, so one exchanges a physical body for a heavenly body, and so on up to the planes of Pratyeka-Buddhas, Bodhisattvas and Buddhas. But all alike are things sought by you or abandoned by you; hence the differences between them. How is it possible that the original and essential nature of the universe should be subject to this differentiation?

*   *   *

21. Q: How do the Buddhas, out of their vast mercy and compassion, preach the Dharma (*Law*) to sentient beings?

A: We speak of their mercy and compassion as vast just because it is beyond causality (*and therefore infinite*). By mercy is really meant not conceiving of a Buddha to be Enlightened, while compassion really means not conceiving of sentient beings to be delivered.[1]

[1] The Zen Masters, in their single-minded desire to lead their disciples beyond the realm of dualism, would have them abandon even the

In reality, their Dharma is neither preached in words nor otherwise signified; and those who listen neither hear nor attain. It is as though an imaginary teacher had preached to imaginary people. As regards all these dharmas (*teachings*), if, for the sake of the Way, I speak to you from my deeper knowledge and lead you forward, you will certainly be able to understand what I say; and, as to mercy and compassion, if for your sakes I take to thinking things out and studying other people's concepts—in neither case will you have reached a true perception of the real nature of your own Mind from WITHIN YOURSELVES. So, in the end, these things will be of no help at all.

*   *   *

22. Q: What is the meaning of 'zealous application'?[2]

A: The most completely successful form of zealous application is the absence from your minds of all such distinctions as 'my body', 'my mind'. As soon as you begin to seek for something outside your own Mind, you are like Kalirāja bent on hunting.[3] But when you prevent your minds from going on travels outside themselves, you are already a kṣānti-rishi. NO BODIES AND NO MINDS—that is the Way of the Buddhas!

*   *   *

notion of compassion as such, since it leads to the dualistic concept of its opposite. By Zen adepts compassion must be practised as a matter o. course and without giving rise to the least feeling of self-satisfaction Still less may it be practised as a means of gaining some heavenly or earthly reward.

[2] One of the six pāramitās.

[3] Kalirāja is said to have sliced up some sages, including a former incarnation of Gautama Buddha. The latter bore this piecemeal dismemberment with the equanimity of a kṣānti-rishi, one who practises the pāramitā of uncomplaining patience in affliction.

23. Q: If I follow this Way, and refrain from intellectual processes and conceptual thinking, shall I be certain of attaining the goal?

A: Such non-intellection IS following the Way! Why this talk of attaining and not attaining? The matter is thus—by thinking of something you create an entity and by thinking of nothing you create another. Let such erroneous thinking perish utterly, and then nothing will remain for you to go seeking!

*　　　*　　　*

24. Q: What is meant by 'Transcending the Three Worlds'? (*Of desire, form and formlessness.*)[1]

A: Transcending the Three Worlds connotes rising beyond the dualism of good and evil. Buddhas appear in the world in order to make an end of desire, of form and of formless phenomena. For you also the Three Worlds will vanish if you can reach the state beyond thought. On the other hand, if you still cling to the notion that something, even if it be as small as the hundredth part of a grain, might exist objectively, then even a perfect mastery of the entire Mahāyāna Canon will fail to give you victory over the Three Worlds. Only when every one of those tiny fragments is seen to be nothing can the Mahāyāna achieve this victory for you.[2]

*　　　*　　　*

[1] The formless world is far other than the Great Void, being one of the three states or worlds constituting saṁsāra.

[2] I.e. even atoms have no objective existence—whether atoms of matter or those atoms of consciousness in which certain Buddhist metaphysicians believed.

25. One day, after taking his seat in the great hall, the Master began as follows. Since Mind is the Buddha (*Absolute*), it embraces all things, from the Buddhas (*Enlightened Beings*) at one extreme to the meanest of belly-crawling reptiles or insects at the other. All these alike share the Buddha-Nature and all are of the substance of the One Mind. So, after his arrival from the West, Bodhidharma transmitted naught but the Dharma of the One Mind. He pointed directly to the truth that all sentient beings have always been of one substance with the Buddha. He did not follow any of those mistaken 'methods of attainment'. And if YOU could only achieve this comprehension of your own Mind, thereby discovering your real nature, there would assuredly be nothing for you to seek, either.

*   *   *

26. Q: How, then, does a man accomplish this comprehension of his own Mind?

A: That which asked the question IS your own Mind; but if you were to remain quiescent and to refrain from the smallest mental activity, its substance would be seen as a void—you would find it formless, occupying no point in space and falling neither into the category of existence nor into that of non-existence. Because it is imperceptible, Bodhidharma said: 'Mind, which is our real nature, is the unbegotten and indestructible Womb; in response to circumstances, it transforms itself into phenomena. For the sake of convenience, we speak of Mind as the intelligence; but when it does not respond to circumstances,[1] it cannot be spoken of in such dualistic terms as existence or non-

[1] And so rests from creating objects.

87

existence. Besides, even when engaged in creating objects in response to causality, it is still imperceptible. If you know this and rest tranquilly in nothingness—then you are indeed following the Way of the Buddhas. Therefore does the sūtra say: 'Develop a mind which rests on no thing whatever.'

Every one of the sentient beings bound to the wheel of alternating life and death is re-created from the karma of his own desires! Endlessly their hearts remain bound to the six states of existence, thereby involving them in all sorts of sorrow and pain. Ch'ing Ming[1] says: 'There are people with minds like those of apes who are very hard to teach; people who need all sorts of precepts and doctrines with which to force their hearts into submission.' And so when thoughts arise, all sorts of dharmas[2] follow, but they vanish with thought's cessation. We can see from this that every sort of dharma is but a creation of Mind. And all kinds of beings—humans, devas, sufferers in hell, asuras and all comprised within the six forms of life—each one of them is Mind-created. If only you would learn how to achieve a state of non-intellection, immediately the chain of causation would snap.

Give up those erroneous thoughts leading to false distinctions! There is no 'self' and no 'other'. There is no 'wrong desire', no 'anger', no 'hatred', no 'love', no 'victory', no 'failure'. Only renounce the error of intellectual or conceptual thought-processes and your nature will exhibit its pristine purity—for this alone is the way to attain Enlightenment, to observe the Dharma (*Law*), to become a Buddha and all the rest. Unless you understand this, the

[1] A famous lay-disciple.
[2] Doctrines, precepts, concepts, things.

whole of your great learning, your painful efforts to advance, your austerities of diet and clothing, will not help you to a knowledge of your own Mind. All such practices must be termed fallacious, for any of them will lead to your rebirth among 'demons'—enemies of the truth—or among the crude nature spirits. What end is served by pursuits like those? Chih Kung says: 'Our bodies are the creations of our own minds.' But how can one expect to gain such knowledge from books? If only you could comprehend the nature of your own Mind and put an end to discriminatory thought, there would naturally be no room for even a grain of error to arise. Ch'ing Ming expressed this in a verse:

> Just spread out a mat
> For reclining quite flat—
> When thought's tied to a bed
> Like a sick man growing worse.
> All karma will cease
> And all fancies disperse.
> THAT's what is meant by Bodhi!

As it is, so long as your mind is subject to the slightest movement of thought, you will remain engulfed in the error of taking 'ignorant' and 'Enlightened' for separate states; this error will persist regardless of your vast knowledge of the Mahāyāna or of your ability to pass through the 'Four Grades of Sainthood' and the 'Ten Stages of Progress Leading to Enlightenment'. For all these pursuits belong to what is ephemeral; even the most strenuous of your efforts is doomed to fail, just as an arrow shot never so high into the air must inevitably fall spent to the ground. So, in spite of them, you are certain to find yourselves back on the wheel of life and death. Indulging in such practices implies your failure to understand the Buddha's real meaning. Surely the endurance of so much unnecessary suffering is nothing but a gigantic error, isn't it? Chih Kung says elsewhere: 'If you do not meet with a teacher able to transcend the worlds, you will go on swallowing the medicine of the Mahāyāna Dharma quite in vain.'

Were you now to practise keeping your minds motionless at all times, whether walking, standing, sitting or lying; concentrating entirely upon the goal of no thought-creation, no duality, no reliance on others and no attachments; just allowing all things to take their course the whole day long, as though you were too ill to bother; unknown to the world; innocent of any urge to be known or unknown to others; with your minds like blocks of stone that mend no holes—then all the Dharmas[1] would penetrate your understanding through and through. In a little while you would find yourselves firmly unattached. Thus, for the first time in your lives, you would discover your reactions to phenomena decreasing and, ultimately, you would pass beyond the Triple World; and people would say that a Buddha had appeared in the world. Pure and passionless knowledge[2] implies putting an end to the ceaseless flow of thoughts and images, for in that way you stop creating the karma that leads to rebirth—whether as gods or men or as sufferers in hell.

Once every sort of mental process has ceased, not a particle of karma is formed. Then, even in this life, your minds and bodies become those of a being completely

[1] Laws of Existence or Universal Laws.
[2] Enlightenment.

liberated. Supposing that this does not result in freeing you immediately from further rebirths, at the very least you will be assured of rebirth in accordance with your own wishes. The sūtra declares: 'Bodhisattvas are re-embodied into whatsoever forms they desire.' But were they suddenly to lose the power of keeping their minds free from conceptual thought, attachment to form would drag them back into the phenomenal world, and each of those forms would create for them a demon's karma!

With the practices of the Pure Land Buddhists it is also thus, for all these practices are productive of karma; hence, we may call them Buddha-hindrances! As they would obstruct your Mind, the chain of causation would also grapple you fast, dragging you back into the state of those as yet unliberated.[1]

Hence all dharmas such as those purporting to lead to the attainment of Bodhi possess no reality. The words of Gautama Buddha were intended merely as efficacious expedients for leading men out of the darkness of worse ignorance. It was as though one pretended yellow leaves were gold to stop the flow of a child's tears. Samyak-Saṁbodhi[2] is another name for the realization that there are no valid Dharmas. Once you understand this, of what use are such trifles to you? According harmoniously with

[1] The Pure Land Sect advocates utter reliance upon Amida, Buddha of Boundless Light and Life, holding that perfect faith will ensure rebirth in a paradise where preparation for final Enlightenment follows under ideal conditions. Zen Buddhists, on the contrary, often claim that reliance on Amida Buddha is the negation of that self-reliance which Gautama Buddha taught to be the only sure path. Nevertheless, the Pure Land doctrine PROPERLY UNDERSTOOD is not truly opposed to Zen, since the real meaning of Amida is the Buddha-Substance innate in man, and rebirth into his paradise implies the awakening of the individual's mind to its Oneness with the Buddha-Substance.

[2] Supreme Knowledge.

the conditions of your present lives, you should go on, as opportunities arise, reducing the store of old karma laid up in previous lives; and above all, you must avoid building up a fresh store of retribution for yourselves!

Mind is filled with radiant clarity, so cast away the darkness of your old concepts. Ch'ing Ming says: 'Rid yourselves of everything.' The sentence in the Lotus Sūtra concerning a whole twenty years spent in the shovelling away of manure symbolizes the necessity of driving from your minds whatever tends to the formation of concepts. In another passage, the same sūtra identifies the pile of dung which has to be carted away with metaphysics and sophistry. Thus the 'Womb of the Tathāgatas' is intrinsically a voidness and silence containing no individualized dharmas of any sort or kind. And therefore says the sūtra: 'The entire realms of all the Buddhas are equally void.'[1]

Though others may talk of the Way of the Buddhas as something to be reached by various pious practices and by sūtra-study, you must have nothing to do with such ideas. A perception, sudden as blinking, that subject and object are one, will lead to a deeply mysterious wordless understanding; and by this understanding will you awake to the truth of Zen. When you happen upon someone who has no understanding, you must claim to know nothing. He may be delighted by his discovery of some 'way to Enlightenment'; yet if you allow yourselves to be persuaded by him, YOU will experience no delight at all, but suffer both sorrow and disappointment. What have such thoughts as his to do with the study of Zen? Even if you do obtain from him some trifling 'method', it will only be a thought-

[1] The implication is that the Western Paradise of Amida Buddha is as void as the rest of them.

constructed dharma having nothing to do with Zen. Thus, Bodhidharma sat rapt in meditation before a wall; he did not seek to lead people into having opinions. Therefore it is written: 'To put out of mind even the principle from which action springs is the true teaching of the Buddhas, while dualism belongs to the sphere of demons.'

Your true nature is something never lost to you even in moments of delusion, nor is it gained at the moment of Enlightenment. It is the Nature of the Bhūtatathatā. In it is neither delusion nor right understanding. It fills the Void everywhere and is intrinsically of the substance of the One Mind. How, then, can your mind-created objects exist outside the Void? The Void is fundamentally without spacial dimensions, passions, activities, delusions or right understanding. You must clearly understand that in it there are no things, no men and no Buddhas; for this Void contains not the smallest hairsbreadth of anything that can be viewed spacially; it depends on nothing and is attached to nothing. It is all-pervading, spotless beauty; it is the self-existent and uncreated Absolute. Then how can it even be a matter for discussion that the REAL Buddha has no mouth and preaches no Dharma, or that REAL hearing requires no ears, for who could hear it? Ah, it is a jewel beyond all price![1]

---

[1] This passage, in which the Master comes as near as possible to describing the indescribable, using terms as 'all-pervading spotless beauty', should be sufficient answer to those critics of Buddhist 'pessimism' who suppose that the doctrine of śūnyatā or voidness equates Nirvāna with total extinction.

THE ANECDOTES

27. Our Master came originally from Fukien, but took his vows upon Mount Huang Po in this prefecture while he was still very young.[1] In the centre of his forehead was a small lump shaped like a pearl. His voice was soft and agreeable, his character unassuming and placid.

Some years after his ordination, while journeying to Mount T'ien T'ai, he fell in with a monk with whom he soon came to feel like an old acquaintance; so they continued their journey together. Finding the way barred by a mountain stream in flood, our Master lent upon his staff and halted, at which his friend entreated him to proceed.

'No. You go first,' said our Master. So the former floated his big straw rain-hat on the torrent and easily made his way to the other side.[2]

'I,' sighed the Master, 'have allowed such a fellow to accompany me! I ought to have slain him with a blow of my staff!'[3]

*   *   *

28. Once a certain monk, on taking leave of Master Kuei Tsung, was asked where he intended to go.

---

[1] It was from this mountain that the Venerable Hsi Yün received the name by which he has been most commonly known until today.

[2] Using it as a raft.

[3] This anecdote seems to mean that the other monk was displaying one of the supranormal powers which dhyāna-practice brings in its train but which should properly be regarded as mere by-products never to be used except in case of dire necessity. Huang Po was clearly disgusted with his companion for showing off.

'I intend to visit all the places where the five kinds of Zen are taught,' he replied.

'Oh,' exclaimed Kuei Tsung. 'Other places may have five kinds; here we have only the one kind.'

But when the monk enquired what it was, he received a sudden blow. 'I see, I see!' he shouted excitedly.

'Speak, speak!' roared Kuei Tsung. So the monk got ready to say something further, but just at that moment he received another blow.

Afterwards, this same monk arrived at our Master's monastery and, being asked by Huang Po where he had come from, explained that he had recently left Kuei Tsung.

'And what instructions did you receive from him?' enquired our Master, whereupon the monk related the above story.

During the next assembly, our Master took this anecdote for his text and said: 'Master Ma[1] really excels the Eighty-Four Deeply Enlightened Ones! The questions people ask are all of them no better than stinking muck saturating the ground. There is only Kuei Tsung who is worth something.'[2]

*   *   *

29. Our Master once attended an assembly at the Bureau of the Imperial Salt Commissioners at which the

[1] Another name for Kuei Tsung.

[2] Those familiar with Dr. Suzuki's books on Zen will not misinterpret Kuei Tsung's blows as being due to unnecessary crudeness or violence, nor Huang Po's strong language as being gratuitously rude. It seems that blows and strong language delivered at the right moment may induce SATORI, a flash of Enlightenment. The younger monk was in search of methods of withdrawal from the world by means of deep contemplation, and Kuei Tsung's first blow was intended as an antidote, for it implied: 'The hand of bone and muscle which now causes you pain is as truly the Absolute as the mystic fervour you experience during contemplation.' The second blow illustrated the folly of trying to express a sudden understanding of truth in words.

Emperor T'ai Chung was also present as a śramanera.[1] The śramanera noticed our Master enter the hall of worship and make a triple prostration to the Buddha, whereupon he asked: 'If we are to seek nothing from the Buddha, Dharma or Saṅgha, what does Your Reverence seek by such prostrations?'

'Though I seek not from the Buddha,' replied our Master, 'or from the Dharma, or from the Saṅgha, it is my custom to show respect in this way.'

'But what purpose does it serve?' insisted the śramanera, whereupon he suddenly received a slap.

'Oh,' he exclaimed. 'How uncouth you are!'

'What is this?' cried the Master. 'Imagine making a distinction between refined and uncouth!' So saying, he administered another slap, causing the śramanera to betake himself elsewhere![2]

*　　　*　　　*

30. During his travels, our Master paid a visit to Nan Ch'üan (*his senior*). One day at dinner-time, he took his bowl and seated himself opposite Nan Ch'üan's high chair.

[1] Here, probably, meaning a layman who had taken ten precepts instead of the normal five.

[2] This story is, to anyone familiar with the customs of Eastern courts, hair-raising. That Huang Po should have dared to slap the Divine Emperor, the Son of Heaven, indicates both the immensity of the Master's personal prestige and the utter fearlessness which results logically from an unshakeable conviction that saṁsāric life is but a dream. The Emperor's willingness to accept the blow without retaliation indicates the depth of his admiration for the Master. It must be remembered that Huang Po, as one of several Masters belonging to a relatively small sect, with no temporal authority whatever, cannot be compared to a Western pope or archbishop who, under certain circumstances, might be able to strike a reigning emperor with impunity by reason of his authority as a Prince of the Church.

Noticing him there, Nan Ch'üan stepped down to receive him and asked: 'How long has Your Reverence been following the Way?'

'Since before the era of Bhisma Rāja,' came the reply.[1]

'Indeed?' exclaimed Nan Ch'üan. 'It seems that Master Ma[2] has a worthy grandson[3] here.' Our Master then walked quietly away.

A few days later, when our Master was going out, Nan Ch'üan remarked: 'You are a huge man, so why wear a hat of such ridiculous size?'

'Ah, well,' replied our Master. 'It contains vast numbers of chiliocosms.'

'Well, what of me?' enquired Nan Ch'üan, but the Master put on his hat and walked off.[4]

*　　　　*　　　　*

[1] This implies that he had been upon the Way since many aeons before the present world cycle began—an allusion to the eternity in which we all share by reason of our identity with the One Mind.

[2] Nan Ch'üan himself.

[3] Spiritual descendant.

[4] Just as the first part of the anecdote implies coexistence with eternity, so the second demonstrates coextensiveness with the Void. When the Master walks away, he implies that he has had the better of the argument. As will be seen, he acknowledges defeat with a triple prostration. Japanese commentators incline to the view that Huang Po's famous hat was too big even for him; but the Chinese, rightly I think, take it that the hat was much too small—which, of course, adds to the point of the story. The words of the text are 'TAI KO HSIEH-TZŬ TA LI'—'wear one tiny-sized hat'; but the word TA, meaning 'size' or 'sized' also commonly means 'big'. Hence the error, which is more understandable inasmuch as HSIEH-TZŬ—'tiny'—is a highly colloquial Chinese term which probably means something quite different in Japanese. *See beneath:*

戴簡些子大笠

31. Another day, our Master was seated in the tea-room when Nan Ch'üan came down and asked him: 'What is meant by "A clear insight into the Buddha-Nature results from the study of dhyāna (*mind control*) and prajñā (*wisdom*)"?'

Our Master replied: 'It means that, from morning till night, we should never rely on a single thing.'

'But isn't that just Your Reverence's own concept of its meaning?

'How could I be so presumptuous?'

'Well, Your Reverence, some people might pay out cash for rice-water, but whom could you ask to give anything for a pair of home-made straw sandals like that?'

At this our Master remained silent.

Later, Wei Shan mentioned the incident to Yang Shan, enquiring if our Master's silence betokened defeat.

'Oh no!' answered Yang. 'Surely you know that Huang Po has a tiger's cunning?'

'Indeed there's no limit to your profundity,' exclaimed the other.[1]

*   *   *

32. Once our Master requested a short leave of absence and Nan Shan asked where he was going.

'I'm just off to gather some vegetables.'

'What are you going to cut them with?'

---

[1] Nan Ch'üan had made use of a term which was anathema to Huang Po—'concept'. His silence was deeply significant; it implied that the Master NEVER indulged in concepts; and, perhaps, further, that 'Your Reverence's' in the sense of 'your' was also a term without validity. But it took a man of Yang Shan's calibre to penetrate through to his meaning.

Our Master held up his knife, whereupon Nan Shan remarked: 'Well, that's all right for a guest but not for a host.'

Our Master showed his appreciation with a triple prostration.[1]

*   *   *

33. One day, five new arrivals presented themselves to our Master in a group. One of them, instead of making the customary prostration, remained standing and greeted him somewhat casually with a motion of his clasped hands.

'And do you know how to be a good hunting-dog?' enquired our Master.

'I must follow the antelope's scent.'

'Suppose it leaves no scent, what will you follow then?'

'Then I'd follow its hoof-marks.'

'And if there were no hoof-marks, what then?'

'I could still follow the animal's tracks.'

'But what if there were not even tracks? How would you follow it then?'

'In that case,' said the newcomer, 'it would surely be a dead antelope.'

Our Master said nothing more at the time but, on the following morning after his sermon, he asked: 'Will yesterday's antelope-hunting monk now step forward.' The monk complied and our Master enquired: 'Yesterday, my

---

[1] I find this anecdote hard to understand. Even the Zen Master Jên Wên, who experienced little difficulty in answering my other questions, remained silent over this one. So I am forced to venture my own guess, which is that the operative sentence means 'Well, by all means use it, but don't let it use you', implying THAT ONLY CAUTIOUS AND TEMPORARY USE SHOULD BE MADE OF ANY EXTERNAL MEANS TO ENLIGHTENMENT. This, whether a good interpretation or not, is at any rate one of Huang Po's most firmly held opinions.

Reverend friend, you were left without anything to say. How was that?'

Finding that the other returned no answer, he continued: 'Ah, you may call yourself a real monk, but you are just an amateur novice.'[1]

*   *   *

34. Once, when our Master had just dismissed the first of the daily assemblies at the K'ai Yuan Monastery near Hung Chou, I[2] happened to enter its precincts. Presently I noticed a wall-painting and, by questioning the monk in charge of the monastery's administration, learnt that it portrayed a certain famous monk.

'Indeed?' I said. 'Yes, I can see his likeness before me, but where is the man himself?' My question was received in silence.[3]

So I remarked: 'But surely there ARE Zen monks here in this temple, aren't there?'

'Yes,' replied the monastery administrator, 'THERE IS ONE.[4]

After that, I requested an audience with the Master and repeated to him my recent conversation.

[1] Huang Po's opening remark implies that he was ready to accord the newcomer the equality tacitly demanded by his casual manner of greeting, PROVIDED he showed himself worthy. It was not until the other had displayed his ignorance of Zen that the Master decided upon a reproof in public. The antelope, of course, symbolizes the One Mind which, being utterly devoid of attributes, 'leaves no tracks'. A dead antelope would imply a state of extinction.

[2] P'ei Hsiu.

[3] Silence indicating that the man was neither anywhere nor nowhere; the first, because his real 'Self' was no special entity; the second, because his ephemeral 'self' undoubtedly occupied a point in space.

[4] This profound reply has a double meaning—'one' in the sense of Huang Po, and 'One'!

'P'ei Hsiu!' cried the Master.

'Sir!' I answered respectfully.

'Where are YOU?'

Realizing that no reply was possible to such a question, I hastened to ask our Master to re-enter the hall and continue his sermon.

*　　　*　　　*

35.[1] When the Master had taken his place in the assembly hall, he began:

'You people are just like drunkards. I don't know how you manage to keep on your feet in such a sodden condition. Why, everyone will die of laughing at you. It all seems so EASY, so why do we have to live to see a day like this? Can't you understand that in the whole Empire of T'ang[2] there are NO "teachers skilled in Zen"?'

At this point, one of the monks present asked: 'How can you say that? At this very moment, as all can see, we are sitting face to face with one who has appeared in the world[3] to be a teacher of monks and a leader of men!'

'Please note that I did not say there is no ZEN,' answered our Master. 'I merely pointed out that there are no TEACHERS!'

Later, Wei Shan reported this conversation to Yang Shan and asked what it implied.

Said Yang Shan: 'That swan is able to extract the pure milk from the adulterated mixture. It is very clear that he[4] is not just an ordinary duck!'

[1] A continuation of 34.
[2] China.
[3] A phrase normally used of Buddhas.
[4] Huang Po.

'Ah,' responded the other. 'Yes, the point he made was very subtle.'[1]

*　　　　*　　　　*

36. One day I brought a statue of the Buddha and, kneeling respectfully before our Master, begged him to bestow upon me a sacred honorific.

'P'ei Hsiu!' he cried.

'Yes, Master?'

'How is it that you still concern yourself with names?'

All I could do was to prostrate myself in silence.

And there was another time when I offered our Master a poem I had written. He took it in his hands, but soon sat down and pushed it away. 'Do you understand?' he asked.

'No, Master.'

'But WHY don't you understand? Think a little! If things could be expressed like this with ink and paper, what would be the purpose of a sect like ours?'

My poem ran as follows:

> When his Master bequeathed him Mind-Intuition,
> He of great height with a pearl on his forehead
> Dwelt for ten years by the river in Szech'uan.
> Now, like a chalice borne by the waters,

---

[1] The implications of this anecdote are manifold. Huang Po's final remark implies among other things the impossibility of TEACHING Zen, which can only be properly apprehended through intuitive understanding arising from within ourselves. Another implication, harking back to the silence of the monastery administrator, is that the existence of INDIVIDUALS, Zen Masters or otherwise, is of a purely transitory order. Absorption in Zen leads to an experience of unity in which 'one' and 'other' are no longer valid. The One is neither a Zen Master nor anything else.

He has come to rest on the banks of the Chang.
A thousand disciples follow behind him
With dragon-mien glorious, bearing the fragrance
Of flowers from afar. These are aspirant Buddhas,
Yet desiring to serve him humbly as pupils.
Who knows upon which the Transmission will fall?

Our Master later replied with another poem:

Mind is a mighty ocean, a sea which knows no bounds.
Words are but scarlet lotus to cure the lesser ills.
Though there be times of leisure when my hands both lie at rest,
'Tis not to welcome idlers that I raise them to my breast![1]

*   *   *

37. Our Master said: Those who desire progress along the Way must first cast out the dross acquired through heterogeneous learning. Above all, they must avoid seeking for anything objective or permitting themselves any sort of attachment. Having listened to the profoundest doctrines, they must behave as though a light breeze had caressed their ears, a gust had passed away in the blink of an eye. By no means may they attempt to follow such doctrines. To act in accordance with these injunctions is to achieve profundity. The motionless contemplation of the Tathāgatas implies the Zen-mindedness of one who has left the round of birth and death forever. From the days when Bodhidharma first transmitted naught but the One Mind, there

[1] Huang Po's poem implies that the Transmission can fall only upon one who has received intuitive experience leading to a direct perception of the One Mind. Mere intellectual brilliance will avail nothing. Hence, to those who idle away their time in metaphysical or intellectual discussions, the Master will make no sign.

has been no other valid Dharma. Pointing to the identity of Mind and the Buddha,[1] he demonstrated how the highest forms of Enlightenment could be transcended. Assuredly he left no other thought but this. If you wish to enter by the gate of our sect, this must be your only Dharma.

If you expect to gain anything from teachers of other doctrines, what is your purpose in coming here? So it is said that if you have the merest intention to indulge in conceptual thinking, behold, your very intention will place you in the clutch of demons. Similarly, a conscious lack of such intention, or even a consciousness that you do NOT have NO such intention, will be sufficient to deliver you into the demons' power. But they will not be demons from outside; they will be the self-creations of your own mind. The only reality is that 'Bodhisattva' whose existence is totally unmanifested even in a spiritual sense—the Trackless One. If ever you should allow yourselves to believe in the more than purely transitory existence of phenomena, you will have fallen into a grave error known as the heretical belief in eternal life; but if, on the contrary, you take the intrinsic voidness of phenomena to imply mere emptiness, then you will have fallen into another error, the heresy of total extinction.[2]

Thus, 'the Triple World is only Mind; the myriad phenomena are only consciousness' is the sort of thing taught to people who previously maintained even falser views and suffered from even graver errors of perception.[3] Similarly,

[1] Absolute.

[2] Since we are compounded, in truth, wholly of eternal Mind, the notion of a permanent individual soul and that of total extinction are equally false.

[3] In Huang Po's time there was a sect called the Wei Shih Tsung which held that, though nothing exists outside consciousness, the latter is in some sense a substance and therefore 'real'.

the doctrine that the Dharmakāya[1] is something attained only after reaching full Enlightenment was merely intended as a means of converting the Theravādin saints from graver errors. Finding these mistaken views prevalent, Gautama Buddha refuted two sorts of misunderstanding—the notions that Enlightenment will lead to the perception of a universal substance, composed of particles which some hold to be gross and others subtle.[2]

How is it possible that Gautama Buddha, who denied all such views as those I have mentioned, could have originated the present conceptions of Enlightenment? But, as these doctrines are still commonly taught, people become involved in the duality of longing for 'light' and eschewing 'darkness'. In their anxiety to SEEK Enlightenment on the one hand and to ESCAPE from the passions and ignorance of corporeal existence on the other, they conceive of an Enlightened Buddha and unenlightened sentient beings as separate entities. Continued indulgence in such dualistic concepts as these will lead to your rebirth among the six orders of beings, life after life, aeon upon aeon, forever and forever! And why is it thus? Because of falsifying the doctrine that the original source of the Buddhas is that self-existent Nature. Let me assure you again that the Buddha dwells not in light, nor sentient beings in darkness, for the Truth allows no such distinctions. The Buddha is not mighty, nor sentient beings feeble, for the Truth allows no such distinctions. The Buddha is not

[1] The body of the Absolute.
[2] These views, which the Buddha is said to have refuted, would seem to be similar to the new scientific theory that the stuff of the universe is mind-stuff. This theory bears a certain superficial resemblance to Huang Po's doctrine; yet, though it is doubtless an advance on the materialistic conception of the last century, it stops far short of the truth as understood in Zen.

Enlightened, nor sentient beings ignorant, for the Truth allows no such distinctions. It is all because you take it upon yourself to talk of EXPLAINING Zen!

As soon as the mouth is opened, evils spring forth. People either neglect the root and speak of the branches, or neglect the reality of the 'illusory' world and speak only of Enlightenment. Or else they chatter of cosmic activities leading to transformations, while neglecting the Substance from which they spring—indeed, there is NEVER any profit in discussion.

Once more, ALL phenomena are basically without existence, though you cannot now say that they are NON-EXISTENT. Karma having arisen does not thereby exist; karma destroyed does not thereby cease to exist. Even its root does not exist, for that root is no root. Moreover, Mind is not Mind, for whatever that term connotes is far from the reality it symbolizes. Form, too, is not really form. So if I now state that there are no phenomena and no Original Mind, you will begin to understand something of the intuitive Dharma silently conveyed to Mind with Mind. Since phenomena and no-phenomena are one, there is neither phenomena nor no-phenomena, and the only possible transmission is to Mind with Mind.

When a sudden flash of thought occurs in your mind and you recognize it for a dream or an illusion, then you can enter into the state reached by the Buddhas of the past—not that the Buddhas of the past really exist, or that the Buddhas of the future have not yet come into existence. Above all, have no longing to become a future Buddha; your sole concern should be, as thought succeeds thought, to avoid clinging to any of them. Nor may you entertain the least ambition to be a Buddha here and now. Even if a Buddha arises, do not think of him as 'Enlightened' or 'deluded', 'good' or 'evil'. Hasten to rid yourself of any desire to cling to him. Cut him off in the twinkling of an eye! On no account seek to hold him fast, for a thousand locks could not stay him, nor a hundred thousand feet of rope bind him. This being so, valiantly strive to banish and annihilate him.

I will now make luminously clear how to set about being rid of that Buddha. Consider the sunlight. You may say it is near, yet if you follow it from world to world you will never catch it in your hands. Then you may describe it as far away and, lo, you will see it just before your eyes. Follow it and, behold, it escapes you; run from it and it follows you close. You can neither possess it nor have done with it. From this example you can understand how it is with the true Nature of all things and, henceforth, there will be no need to grieve or to worry about such things.

Now, beware of going on to say that my recommendation to cut off the Buddha was profane, or that my comparing him to the sunshine was pious, as though I had wavered from the one extreme to the other! Followers of the other sects would then agree with you, but our Zen Sect will not admit either the profanity of the first nor the pious quality of the second. Nor do we regard the first as Buddha-like, or the second as something to be expected only from ignorant sentient beings.[1]

Thus all the visible universe IS the Buddha; so are all

---

[1] The whole of this passage is a warning against one of the most difficult types of dualism for a Buddhist to avoid—the dualism involved in conceiving of the Buddha or Nirvāṇa as separate from ourselves and saṁsāra. An attempt to blot out the Buddha is no more impious than the attempt to murder a stone image, since both are impervious to such designs.

sounds; hold fast to one principle and all the others are Identical. On seeing one thing, you see ALL. On perceiving any individual's mind, you are perceiving ALL Mind. Obtain a glimpse of one way and ALL ways are embraced in your vision, for there is nowhere at all which is devoid of the Way. When your glance falls upon a grain of dust, what you see is identical with all the vast world-systems with their great rivers and mighty hills. To gaze upon a drop of water is to behold the nature of all the waters of the universe. Moreover, in thus contemplating the totality of phenomena, you are contemplating the totality of Mind. All these phenomena are intrinsically void and yet this Mind with which they are identical is no mere nothingness. By this I mean that it does exist, but in a way too marvellous for us to comprehend. It is an existence which is no existence, a non-existence which is nevertheless existence. So this true Void does in some marvellous way 'exist'.[1]

According to what has been said, we can encompass all the vast world-systems, though numberless as grains of sand, with our One Mind. Then, why talk of 'inside' and 'outside'? Honey having the invariable characteristic of sweetness, it follows that all honey is sweet. To speak of this honey as sweet and that honey as bitter would be nonsensical! How COULD it be so? Hence we say that the Void has no inside and outside. There is only the spontaneously existing Bhūtatathatā (*Absolute*). And, for this same reason, we say it has no centre. There is only the spontaneously existing Bhūtatathatā.

Thus, sentient beings ARE the Buddha. The Buddha is one with them. Both consist entirely of the one 'substance'.

[1] This passage emphasizes the perfect identity of Nirvāṇa's matchless calm with the restless flux of the phenomenal universe.

The phenomenal universe and Nirvāṇa, activity and motionless placidity—ALL are of the one 'substance'. So also are the worlds and with the state that transcends worlds. Yes, the beings passing through the six stages of existence, those who have undergone the four kinds of birth, all the vast world-systems with their mountains and river, the Bodhi-Nature and illusion—ALL of them are thus. By saying that they are all of one substance, we mean that their names and forms, their existence and non-existence, are void. The great world-systems, uncountable as Gangā's sands, are in truth comprised in the one boundless void. Then where CAN there be Buddhas who deliver or sentient beings to be delivered? When the true nature of all things that 'exist' is an identical Thusness, how CAN SUCH distinctions have any reality?

If you suppose that phenomena arise of themselves, you will fall into the heresy of regarding things as having a spontaneous existence of their own. On the other hand, if you accept the doctrine of ANĀTMAN, the concept 'ANĀTMAN' may land you among the Theravādins.[1]

---

[1] The doctrine of ANĀTMAN has always been the centre of Buddhist controversy. There is no doubt that Gautama Buddha made it one of the central points of his teaching, but the interpretations of it are various. The Theravādins interpret it not only as 'no self', but also as 'no Self', thereby denying man both an ego and all participation in something of the nature of Universal Spirit or the One Mind. The Mahāyānists accept the interpretation of 'egolessness', holding that the real 'Self' is none other than that indescribable 'non-entity', the One Mind; something far less of an 'entity' than the ĀTMAN of the Brahmins. Coomaraswamy, for example, interprets the famous precept 'Take the self as your only refuge' not by the Theravādin 'Place no reliance upon intermediaries', but by 'Take only the Self as your refuge', the 'Self' meaning the same as the One Mind. If the Theravādins are right with their 'No ego AND no Self', what is it that reincarnates and finally enters Nirvāna? And why do they take such pains to store up merit for future lives? For if the temporarily adhering aggregates of personality are not held together either by an ego-soul or by a Universal Self or the One

You people seek to measure all within the void, foot by foot and inch by inch, I repeat to you that all phenomena are devoid of distinctions of form. Intrinsically they belong to that perfect tranquillity which lies beyond the transitory sphere of form-producing activities, so all of them are coexistent with space and one with reality. Since no bodies possess real form, we speak of phenomena as void; and, since Mind is formless, we speak of the nature of all things as void. Both are formless and both are termed void. Moreover, none of the numerous doctrines has any existence outside your original Mind. All this talk of Bodhi, Nirvāṇa, the Absolute, the Buddha-Nature, Mahāyāna, Theravāda, Bodhisattvas and so on is like taking autumn leaves for gold. To use the symbol of the closed fist: when it is opened, all beings—both gods and men—will perceive there is not a single thing inside. Therefore is it written:

> There's never been a single thing;
> Then where's defiling dust to cling?[2]

If 'there's never been a single thing', past, present and future are meaningless. So those who seek the Way must

Mind, whatever enters Nirvāṇa when those aggregates have finally dispersed can be of no interest to the man who devotes successive lives to attaining that goal. It is also difficult to understand how Buddhism could have swept like a flame across Asia if, at the time of its vast expansion, it had only the cold comfort of the present Theravādin interpretation of ANĀTMAN to offer those in search of a religion by which to live. Zen adepts, like their fellow Mahāyānists, take ANĀTMAN to imply 'no entity to be termed an ego, naught but the One Mind, which comprises all things and gives them their only reality.'

[2] It is recorded in the Sūtra of Hui Nêng, or Wei Lang, that a certain monk likened Mind to a mirror which must be cleansed of the defilements of delusion and passion, thereby involving himself in a duality between the transitory and the real. The two lines just quoted are from Hui Nêng's reply, in which the duality is confuted.

enter it with the suddenness of a knife-thrust. Full understanding of this must come before they can enter. Hence,
though Bodhidharma traversed many countries on his way
from India to China, he encountered only one man, the
Venerable Ko, to whom he could silently transmit the
Mind-Seal, the Seal of your own REAL Mind. Phenomena
are the Seal of Mind, just as the latter is the Seal of phenomena. Whatever Mind is, so also are phenomena—both
are equally real and partake equally of the Dharma-
Nature, which hangs in the void. He who receives an intuition of this truth has become a Buddha and attained to
the Dharma. Let me repeat that Enlightenment cannot
be bodily grasped (*attained perceived, etc.*), for the body is
formless; nor mentally grasped (*etc.*), for the mind is formless; nor grasped (*etc.*), through its essential nature, since
that nature is the Original Source of all things, the real
Nature of all things, permanent Reality, of Buddha! How
can you use the Buddha to grasp the Buddha, formlessness
to grasp formlessness, mind to grasp mind, void to grasp
void, the Way to grasp the Way? In reality, there is nothing
to be grasped (*perceived, attained, conceived, etc.*)—even
not-grasping cannot be grasped. So it is said: 'There is
NOTHING to be grasped.' We simply teach you how to understand your original Mind.

Moreover, when the moment of understanding comes,
do not think in terms of understanding, not understanding
or not not-understanding, for none of these is something to
be grasped. This Dharma of Thusness when 'grasped' is
'grasped', but he who 'grasps' it is no more conscious of
having done so than someone ignorant of it is conscious of
his failure. Ah, this Dharma of Thusness—until now so few
people have come to understand it that it is written: 'In

this world, how few are they who lose their egos!' As for those people who seek to grasp it through the application of some particular principle or by creating a special environment, or through some scripture, or doctrine, or age, or time, or name, or word, or through their six senses—how do they differ from wooden dolls? But if, unexpectedly, one man were to appear, one who formed no concept based on any name or form, I assure you that this man might be sought through world after world, always in vain! His uniqueness would assure him of succeeding to the Patriarch's place and earn for him the name of Śākya-muni's true spiritual son: the conflicting aggregates of his ego-self would have vanished, and he would indeed be the One! Therefore is it written: 'When the King attains to Buddhahood, the princes accordingly leave their home to become monks. Hard is the meaning of this saying! It is to teach you to refrain from seeking Buddhahood, since any SEARCH is doomed to failure. Some madman shrieking on the mountain-top, on hearing the echo far below, may go to seek it in the valley. But, oh, how vain his search! Once in the valley, he shrieks again and straightway climbs to search among the peaks—why, he may spend a thousand rebirths or ten thousand aeons searching for the source of those sounds by following their echoes! How vainly will he breast the troubled waters of life and death! Far better that you make NO sound, for then will there be no echo—and thus it is with the dwellers in Nirvāṇa! No listening, no knowing, no sound, no track, no trace—make yourselves thus and you will be scarcely less than neighbours of Bodhidharma!

*   *   *

38. Q: Pray instruct me concerning the passage in the sūtras denying the existence of a Sword of Thusness in the Royal Treasury.[1]

A: The Royal Treasury is the nature of the Void. Though all the vast world-systems of the universe are contained therein, none of them have existence outside your Mind. Another name for it is the Bodhisattva Treasury of the Great Void. If you speak of it as existing or not existing, or as neither the one nor the other, in every case it becomes a mere ram's horn![2] It is a ram's horn in the sense that you have made it an object of your useless search.

*   *   *

39. Q: But is there not a Sword of Truth within the Royal Treasury?

A: Another ram's horn!

Q: Yet if there is no Sword of Truth why is it written: 'The Prince seized the Sword of Truth from the Royal Treasury and set out upon his conquests'? Why do you tell us nothing of it beyond denying its objective existence?

A: The prince who took the sword connotes a true spiritual son of the Tathāgata; but, if you say that he carried it off, you imply that he DEPRIVED the Treasury of something. What nonsense it is to speak of carrying off a piece of that Void Nature which is the Source of all things! It would appear that, if you have got hold of anything at all, it may be called a collection of rams' horns!

*   *   *

[1] The Sword of Thusness is a MEANS to Enlightenment; the Royal Treasury is the Bhūtatathatā—the Absolute regarded as the Source of all things.
[2] Rams' horns symbolize passions and delusions.

40. Q: When Kāśyapa received the seal of Buddhahood from Gautama Buddha, did he make use of words during its further transmission?

A: Yes.

Q: Then, since he attempted its transmission in words, even he should be included among the people with rams' horns.

A: Kāśyapa obtained a direct self-realization of original Mind, so he is not one of those with horns. Whosoever obtains this direct realization of the Tathāgata Mind, thereby understanding the true identity of the Tathāgata and perceiving his real appearance and real form, can speak to others with the authority of the Buddha's true spiritual son. But Ānanda,[1] though he served his Master for twenty years, was unable to perceive more than his outward appearance and form, and was therefore admonished by the Buddha in these words: 'Those who concentrate entirely upon helping the world cannot escape from among the horned ones.'[2]

*　　　*　　　*

41. Q: What is the meaning of the passage: 'Mañjuśrī stood before Gautama with a drawn sword'?

A: The 'Five Hundred Bodhisattvas' attained knowledge

[1] Gautama Buddha's most loving disciple, whose compassion excelled his wisdom.

[2] This quotation is certainly not intended to belittle Ānanda's compassion, but to indicate that even the most selfless devotion to others is not an actual means to gain deliverance. If deliverance could be attained merely as a result of good works, Ānanda would have earned it many times over. In some Buddhist sects, the chief emphasis is placed on works of piety and charity; in Zen, nobility of heart and deed are prerequisites for followers of the Path, but they do not form part of the Path to Liberation itself.

of their previous lives and discovered how their previous karma had been constructed. This a fable in which the 'Five Hundred' really refers to your five senses. On account of their knowledge of their previous karma, they SOUGHT the Buddha, Bodhisattvahood and Nirvāṇa objectively.[1] It was for this reason that Mañjuśrī took up the Sword of Bodhi and used it to destroy the concept of a tangible Buddha;[2] and it is for this that he is known as the destroyer of human virtues!

Q: What does the Sword really signify?

A: It signifies the apprehension of Mind.

Q: So the Sword used to destroy the concept of a tangible Buddha[3] is the apprehension of Mind. Well, then, if we are able to put an end to such concepts by this means, how is their destruction actually accomplished?

A: You must use that wisdom which comes from non-dualism to destroy your concept-forming, dualistic mentality.

Q: Assuming that the concepts of something perceptible and of Enlightenment as something to be sought can be destroyed by drawing the Sword of Non-Discriminatory Wisdom, where precisely is such a sword to be found?

A: Since non-discriminatory wisdom is the destroyer both of perception and of its opposite, it must also belong to the Non-perceptible.[4]

Q: Knowledge cannot be used to destroy knowledge, nor a sword to destroy a sword.[5]

[1] Forming sense-based concepts.
[2] Absolute.
[3] Absolute.
[4] Non-attainable, non-graspable, etc. Hence the question is pointless.
[5] The questioner seems to have coined a paradox of the kind Huang Po was fond of using, perhaps as an indication of some fancied advancement towards the truth.

A: Sword DOES destroy sword—they destroy each other —and the no sword remains for you to grasp. Knowledge DOES destroy knowledge—this knowledge invalidates that knowledge—and then no knowledge remains for you to grasp. It is as though mother and son perished together.[1]

*　　　*　　　*

42. Q: What is implied by 'seeing into the real Nature'?

A: That Nature and your perception of it are one. You cannot use it to see something over and above itself. That Nature and your hearing of it are one. You cannot use it to hear something over and above itself. If you form a concept of the true nature of anything as being visible or audible, you allow a dharma of distinction to arise. Let me repeat that the perceived cannot perceive. Can there, I ask you, be a head attached to the crown of your head? I will give you an example to make my meaning clearer. Imagine some loose pearls in a bowl, some large globules and some small. Each one is completely unaware of the others and none causes the least obstruction to the rest. During their formation, they did not say: 'Now I am coming into being': and when they begin to decay, they will not say: 'Now I am decaying.' None of the beings born into the six forms of life through the four kinds of birth are exceptions to this rule. Buddhas and sentient creatures have no mutual perception of each other. The four grades of Theravādin adepts who are able to enter Nirvāṇa do not perceive, nor are they perceived by Nirvāṇa. Those

---

[1] This passage is especially profound. Transcendental knowledge invalidates relative knowledge, but the former is then found to be no knowledge in the ordinary sense, for knower and known are seen to be one.

Theravādins who have reached the 'three stages of holiness' and who possess the 'ten excellent characteristics' neither perceive nor are perceived by Enlightenment. So it is with everything else, down to fire and water, or earth and sky. These pairs of elements have no mutual perception of each other. Sentient beings do not ENTER the Dharmadhātu,[1] nor do the Buddhas ISSUE FROM it. There is no coming and going within the Dharmatā,[2] nor anything perceptible (*etc.*). This being so, why this talk of 'I see', 'I hear', 'I receive an intuition through Enlightenment', 'I hear the Dharma from the lips of an Enlightened One', or of 'Buddhas appearing in the world to preach the Dharma'? Kātyāyana was rebuked by Vimalakīrti[3] for using that transitory mentality which belongs to the ephemeral state to transmit the doctrine of the real existence of matter.

I assure you that all things have been free from bondage since the very beginning.[4] So why attempt to EXPLAIN them? Why attempt to purify what has never been defiled?[5] Therefore it is written: 'The Absolute is THUSNESS—how can it be discussed? You people still conceive of Mind as existing or not existing, as pure or defiled, as something to be studied in the way that one studies a piece of categorical knowledge, or as a concept—any of these definitions is sufficient to throw you back into the endless round of birth and death. The man who PERCEIVES things always wants to identify them, to get a hold on them. Those who use their minds like eyes in this way are sure to suppose that

[1] Absolute.
[2] Nature of the Absolute.
[3] Ch'ing Ming.
[4] I.e. they have never really lost their identity with the Absolute.
[5] The then still existent Northern School of Zen taught purification of the mind, but Hui Nêng, followed here by Huang Po, regarded this injunction as implying a dualism of pure and impure.

progress is a matter of stages. If you are that kind of person, you are as far from the truth as earth is far from heaven. Why this talk of 'seeing into your own nature'?

*   *   *

43. Q: You say that our original nature and the act of seeing into it are one and the same. This can only be so if that nature is totally undifferentiated. Pray explain how it is that, even allowing that there are no real objects for us to perceive, nevertheless we do in fact see what is near to us and are unable to see what is far away.

A: This is due to a misunderstanding arising from your own delusions. You cannot argue that the Universal Nature does in fact contain real objects on the grounds that 'no real objects to be perceived' would only be true if there were nothing of the kind we CALL perceptible. The nature of the Absolute is neither perceptible nor imperceptible; and with phenomena it is just the same. But to one who has discovered his real nature, how can there be anywhere or anything separate from it? Thus, the six forms of life arising from the four kinds of birth, together with the great world-systems of the universe with their rivers and mountains, are ALL of one pure substance with our own nature. Therefore is it said: 'The perception of a phenomenon IS the perception of the Universal Nature, since phenomena and Mind are one and the same.' It is only because you cling to outward forms that you come to 'see', 'hear', 'feel' and 'know' things as individual entities. True perception is beyond your powers so long as you indulge in these.[1]

[1] In this passage it is argued that, though individual entities DO exist in a certain superficial sense, they never lose their fundamental oneness.

By such means you will fall among the followers of the usual Mahāyāna and Theravādin doctrines who rely upon deep PERCEPTION to arrive at a true understanding. Therefore they see what is near and fail to see what is far away, but no one on the right path thinks thus. I assure you there is no 'inner' or 'outer', or 'near' or 'far'. The fundamental nature of all phenomena is close beside you, but you do not SEE even that; yet you still go on talking of your inability to see what is far away. What meaning can this sort of talk possibly have?

*　　　*　　　*

44. Q: What guidance does Your Reverence offer to those of us who find all this very difficult to understand?

A: I have NO THING to offer. I have never had anything to offer others. It is because you allow certain people to lead you astray that you are forever SEEKING intuition and SEARCHING for understanding. Isn't this a case of disciples and teachers all falling into the same insoluble muddle? All you need to remember are the following injunctions:

FIRST, LEARN HOW TO BE ENTIRELY UNRECEPTIVE TO SENSATIONS ARISING FROM EXTERNAL FORMS, THEREBY PURGING YOUR BODIES OF RECEPTIVITY TO EXTERNALS.

SECOND, LEARN NOT TO PAY ATTENTION TO ANY DISTINCTIONS BETWEEN THIS AND THAT ARISING FROM YOUR SENSATIONS, THEREBY PURGING YOUR BODIES OF USELESS DISCERNMENTS BETWEEN ONE PHENOMENON AND ANOTHER.

THIRD, TAKE GREAT CARE TO AVOID DISCRIMINATING IN TERMS OF PLEASANT AND UNPLEASANT SENSATIONS, THEREBY PURGING YOUR BODIES OF VAIN DISCRIMINATIONS.

FOURTH, AVOID PONDERING THINGS IN YOUR MIND, THEREBY
PURGING YOUR BODIES OF DISCRIMINATORY COGNITION.[1]

A single moment's dualistic thought is sufficient to drag
you back to the twelvefold chain of causation.[2] It is ignorance which turns the wheel of causation, thereby creating
an endless chain of karmic causes and results. This is the
law which governs our whole lives up to the time of senility
and death.[3]

In this connection, we are told that Sudhana, after
vainly seeking Bodhi in a hundred and ten places within
the twelvefold causal sphere, at last encountered Maitreya
who sent him to Mañjuśrī. Mañjuśrī here represents your
primordial ignorance of reality. If, as thought succeeds
thought, you go on seeking for wisdom outside yourselves,
then there is a continual process of thoughts arising, dying
away and being succeeded by others. And that is why all
you monks go on experiencing birth, old age, sickness and
death—building up karma which produces corresponding
effects. For such is the arising and passing away of the 'five
bubbles' or, in other words, the five skandhas. Ah, could
you but restrain each single thought from arising, then
would the Eighteen Sense Realms[4] be made to vanish! How
godlike, then, your bodily rewards and how exalted the

[1] These are four of the five skandhas or components of sentient being,
namely: rūpa—form; vedanā—reception of sensation; saṃjñā—discernment; saṃskāra—discrimination; and vijñāna—cognition.

[2] The twelve links are: ignorance; consequent entrance into the womb;
consciousness; rebirth; development of the sense organs; contact with
external phenomena; the resulting sensations; the craving for pleasure
to which these give rise, the amassing of pleasure-giving objects, money,
property and so on; the growth of further karma; rebirth; and fresh
experience of the sorrows of decay and death.

[3] Free will is not denied here, for its proper employment can snap the
causal chain—a principle accepted by Buddhists of all sects.

[4] The six sense organs, including the brain, together with their six
objects and six types of sensation.

knowledge that would dawn within your minds! A mind like that could be called the Terrace of the Spirit. But while you remain lost in attachments, you condemn your bodies to be corpses or, as it is sometimes expressed, to be lifeless corpses inhabited by demons!

*   *   *

45. Q: 'Vimalakīrti dwells in silence. Mañjuśrī offers praise.' How can they have really entered the Gateway of Non-Duality?

A: The Gateway of Non-Duality is your original Mind. Speech and silence are relative concepts belonging to the ephemeral sphere. When nothing is said, nothing is manifested.[1] That is why Mañjuśrī offered praise.

Q: Vimalakīrti did not speak. Does this imply that sound is subject to cessation?[2]

A: Speech and silence are one! There is no distinction between them. Therefore is it written: 'Neither the true nature nor the root of Mañjuśrī's hearing are subject to cessation.' Thus, the sound of the Tathāgata's voice is everlasting, nor can there be any such reality as the time before he began to preach or the time after he finished preaching. The preaching of the Tathāgata is identical with the Dharma he taught, for there is no distinction between the preaching and the thing preached; just as there is none between such varied phenomena as the Glorified and Revealed Bodies of a Buddha, the Bodhisattvas, the Śrāvakas, the world-systems with their mountains and rivers, or water, birds, trees, forests and the rest. The

[1] *Cf.* St. John: 'In the beginning was the WORD.'
[2] This seems to mean: Is sound purely saṁsāric? But I am puzzled.

preaching of the Dharma is at one and the same time both vocal and silent. Though one talks the day long, no word is spoken. This being so, only silence belongs to the Essential.

*   *   *

46. Q: Is it true that the Śrāvakas[1] can only merge their forms into the formless sphere which still belongs to the transitory Triple World, and that they are incapable of losing themselves utterly in Bodhi?

A: Yes. Form implies matter. Those saints are only proficient in casting off worldly views and activities, by which means they escape from worldly delusions and afflictions. They cannot lose themselves utterly in Bodhi; thus, there is still the danger that demons may come and pluck them from within the orbit of Bodhi itself. Aloofly seated in their forest dwellings, they perceive the Bodhi-Mind but vaguely. Whereas those who are vowed to become Bodhisattvas and who are already within the Bodhi of the Three Worlds, neither reject nor grasp at anything. Non-grasping, it were vain to seek them upon any plane; non-rejecting, demons will strive in vain to find them.

Nevertheless, with the merest desire to attach yourselves to this or that, a mental symbol is soon formed, such symbols in turn giving rise to all those 'sacred writings' which lead you back to undergo the various kinds of re-birth. So let your symbolic conception be that of a void, for then the wordless teaching of Zen will make itself apparent to you. Know only that you must decide to

[1] Theravādin saints who do not accept the doctrine of void, but follow the literal meaning of the sūtras.

eschew all symbolizing whatever, for by this eschewal is 'symbolized' the Great Void in which there is neither unity nor multiplicity—that Void which is not really void, that Symbol which is no symbol. Then will the Buddhas of all the vast world-systems manifest themselves to you in a flash; you will recognize the hosts of squirming, wriggling sentient beings as no more than shadows! Continents as innumerable as grains of dust will seem no more to you than a single drop in the great ocean. To you, the profoundest doctrines ever heard will seem but dreams and illusions. You will recognize all minds as One and behold all things as One—including those thousands of sacred books and myriads of pious commentaries! All of them are just your One Mind. Could you but cease your groping after forms, all these true perceptions would be yours! Therefore is it written: 'Within the Thusness of the One Mind, the various means to Enlightenment are no more than showy ornaments.'

*　　　*　　　*

47. Q: But what if in previous lives I have behaved like Kalirāja, slicing the limbs from living men?

A: The holy sages tortured by him represent your own Mind, while Kalirāja symbolizes that part of you which goes out SEEKING. Such unkingly behaviour is called lust for personal advantage. If you students of the Way, without making any attempt to live virtuously, just want to make a study of everything you perceive, then how are you different from him?[1] By allowing your gaze to linger

---

[1] This passage is sufficient answer to those critics of Zen who affirm that Zen disregards the necessity for virtuous living. It does not disregard it at all, but does deny that Enlightenment may be gained by it— which is quite a different thing.

on a form, you wrench out the eyes of a sage (*yourself*). And when you linger upon a sound, you slice off the ears of a sage—thus it is with all your senses and with cognition, for their varied perceptions are called slicers.

Q: When we meet all suffering with sagelike patience and avoid all mind-slicing perceptions, that which suffers with resignation surely cannot be the One Mind, for that cannot be subject to the endurance of pain.

A: You are one of those people who force the Un-becoming into conceptual moulds, such as the CONCEPT of patient suffering or the CONCEPT of seeking nothing outside yourself. Thereby you do yourself violence!

Q: When the holy sages were dismembered, were they conscious of pain; and, if among them there were no entities capable of suffering, who or what did suffer?

A: If you are not suffering pain now, what is the point of chiming in like that?[1]

*   *   *

48. Q: Did Dīpaṃkara Buddha[2] attain his intuition of reality within a single five-hundred-year period or not?

A: There is no attaining it within such a period. You must never forget that this so-called 'attaining' of intuition implies neither a withdrawal from daily life nor a SEARCH for Enlightenment. You have just to understand that time-periods have no real existence; hence the attainment of the vital intuition occurs neither within nor without a five-hundred-year period.

---

[1] This curt reply may also mean: 'Why join this assembly to study Zen-liberation, unless the frustration set up by saṃsāric life is painful to you?'
[2] The twenty-fourth predecessor of Gautama Buddha.

Q: Is it not possible to attain the omniscience in which all the events of past, present and future are known to us?

A: There is absolutely NOTHING which can be attained.

Q: How long is a cycle of five hundred yugas?

A: One such period should be ample for you to become a liberated sage. For, when Dīpaṃkara Buddha 'attained' his intuitive knowledge of the Dharma, there was not really a grain of anything attainable.

* * *

49. Q: The sūtras teach that the fettering of passions and illusions produced during millions of kalpas is a sufficient means of obtaining the Dharmakāya, even without going through the stage of being monks. What does this mean?

A: If you practise MEANS of attaining Enlightenment for three myriad aeons but without losing your belief in something really attainable, you will still be as many aeons from your goal as there are grains of sand in the Ganges. But if, by a direct perception of the Dharmakāya's true nature, you grasp it in a flash, you will have reached the highest goal taught in the Three Vehicles. Why? Because the belief that the Dharmakāya can be obtained belongs to the doctrines of those sects which do not understand the truth.

* * *

50. Q: If on perceiving a phenomenon I gain a sudden comprehension of it, is that tantamount to understanding Bodhidharma's meaning?

A: Bodhidharma's mind penetrated even beyond the void.[1]

Q: Then individual objects DO exist?

A: The existence of things as separate entities and not as separate entities are both dualistic concepts. As Bodhidharma said: 'There are separate entities and there are not, but at the same time they are neither the one nor the other, for relativity is transient.' If you disciples cannot get beyond those incorrect orthodox treachings, why do you call yourselves Zen monks? I exhort you to apply yourselves solely to Zen and not to go seeking after wrong methods which only result in a multiplicity of concepts. A man drinking water knows well enough if it is cold or warm. Whether you be walking or sitting, you must restrain all discriminatory thoughts from one moment to the next. If you do not, you will never escape the chain of rebirth.

*　　　*　　　*

51. Q: If the Buddha really dwells in matchless tranquillity beyond the multiplicity of forms, how is it that his body yielded eighty-four pecks of relics?[2]

A: If you really think like that, you are confusing the transitory relics with the real.

Q: Are there really such things as śarīras,[3] or are they the Buddha's accumulated merits?

A: There are no such things. They are not merits.

---

[1] It is not enough to see all things as fleeting shadows. Beyond the void is the Great Void, in which flux is and yet is not flux. The moon or a tree must first be perceived as void and then, in a new sense, as moon or tree.

[2] This rather naïve questioner is confusing the Buddha as synonymous with the Absolute with the historical figure of Gautama.

[3] Buddha-relics.

Q: Then, why is it written: 'The Buddha-relics are ethereal and subtle; the golden ones are indestructible'? What does Your Reverence say to that?

A: If you harbour such beliefs, why call yourself a student of Zen? Can you imagine bones in the Void? The minds of all the Buddhas are one with the Great Void. What bones do you expect to find there?

Q: But if I had actually seen some of these relics, what then?

A: You would have seen the products of your own wrongthinking.

Q: Does Your Reverence have any of those relics? Please let us see them.

A: A true relic would be hard to see! To find it, you would have to crush mighty Mount Sumeru to fine dust, using only your bare hands!

*　　　*　　　*

52. The Master said: Only when your minds cease dwelling upon anything whatsoever will you come to an understanding of the true way of Zen. I may express it thus—the way of the Buddhas flourishes in a mind utterly freed from conceptual thought processes, while discrimination between this and that gives birth to a legion of demons! Finally, remember that from first to last not even the smallest grain of anything perceptible[1] has ever existed or ever will exist.

*　　　*　　　*

53. Q: To whom did the Patriarch silently transmit the Dharma?

[1] Graspable, attainable, tangible, etc.

A: No Dharma was transmitted to anybody.[1]

Q: Then why did the Second Patriarch ask Bodhidharma for the transmission of Mind?

A: If you hold that something was transmitted, you imply that the Second Patriarch reached Mind by SEEKING, but no amount of seeking can ever lead to Mind; so we TALK of only transmitting Mind to you. If you really GET something, you will find yourself back on the wheel of life and death!

*   *   *

54. Q: Did the Buddha pierce right through the primordial darkness of ignorance?

A: Yes. The primordial darkness is the sphere in which every Buddha achieves Enlightenment. Thus, the very sphere in which karma arises may be called a Bodhimandala.[2] Every grain of matter, every appearance is one with Eternal and Immutable Reality! Wherever your foot may fall, you are still within that Sanctuary for Enlightenment, though it is nothing perceptible. I assure you that one who comprehends the truth of 'nothing to be attained' is already seated in the sanctuary where he will gain his Enlightenment.

Q: Is primordial ignorance bright or dark?

A: It is neither. Both terms are dualistic. Primordial ignorance is at once neither bright nor dark; and by 'the non-bright'[3] is just meant that Original Brightness which is above the distinction made between bright and dark. Just this one sentence is enough to give most people a

[1] I.e. the Dharma has always existed in our own Mind; it is only the realization of this which is lacking.

[2] A sanctuary for gaining Enlightenment.

[3] Avidyā or primordial ignorance.

headache! That is why we say the world is full of vexations arising from the transitory phenomena around us.[1]

Though, like Śāriputra, we were all to strain our minds trying to discover a means of liberation, that would be no way to fathom the wisdom and omniscience by which the Buddhas transcend all space. There can be no argument about it. Once when Gautama had measured out three thousand chiliochosms,[2] a Bodhisattva suddenly appeared and passed over them in a single stride. Yet even that prodigious stride failed to cover the width of one pore of Samantabhadra's skin! Now, what sort of mental attainments have you that will help you to study the meaning of that?

Q: But if such things are entirely unlearnable, then why is it written: 'On returning to our Original Nature, we transcend duality; but the relative means form many gates to the truth'?

A: We return to our Original Nature beyond duality, which in fact is also the real nature of the universe of primordial darkness,[3] which again is the Buddha-Nature. The 'relative means forming many gates' applies to Śrāvakas who hold that our universe is subject to becoming and cessation, and to Pratyeka Buddhas who, though acknowledging the infinity of its past, regard it as subject to future destruction; so they all concentrate entirely on the means of overcoming it.[4] But the real Buddhas perceived

---

[1] In the Chinese, the sentence reads very much as follows, for the word meaning primordial darkness or avidyā is itself composed of two characters meaning 'not' and 'bright': 'Not bright both not bright and not dark not bright just is original bright not bright not dark'! Hence the remark about a headache.

[2] Each containing a myriad worlds.

[3] Saṃsāra—THIS world.

[4] As though it were quite a separate entity from the Nirvāṇa which they seek.

that the becoming and destruction of the sentient world are both one with eternity.[1] In another sense, there is no becoming or cessation. To perceive all this is to be truly Enlightened. Thus Nirvāṇa and Enlightenment are one.

When the lotus opened and the universe lay disclosed, there arose the duality of Absolute and sentient world; or, rather, the Absolute appeared in two aspects which, taken together, comprise pure perfection. These aspects are unchanging reality and potential form. For sentient beings, there are such pairs of opposites as becoming and cessation, together with all the others. Therefore, beware of clinging to one half of a pair. Those who, in their singleminded attempt to reach Buddhahood, detest the sentient world, thereby blaspheme all the Buddhas of the universe. The Buddhas, on manifesting themselves in the world, seized dung-shovels to rid themselves of all such rubbish as books containing metaphysics and sophistry.[2]

My advice to you is to rid yourselves of all your previous ideas about STUDYING Mind or PERCEIVING it. When you are rid of them, you will no longer lose yourselves amid sophistries. Regard the process exactly as you would regard the shovelling of dung.

Yes, my advice is to give up all indulgence in conceptual thought and intellectual processes. When such things no longer trouble you, you will unfailingly reach Supreme Enlightenment. On no account make a distinction between the Absolute and the sentient world. As a real student of Ts'ao Hsi Zen,[3] you must make no distinctions of any kind.

[1] I.e. they recognize the identity of 'a moment' and 'forever'.
[2] Gautama Buddha seems to have held the same view of metaphysics, for he steadily refused to answer metaphysical quesions, regarding them as useless distractions from the work of self-Enlightenment.
[3] The subsect to which Huang Po belonged.

From the earliest times the Sages[1] have taught that a minimum of activity is the gateway of their Dharma; so let NO activity be the gateway of my Dharma! Such is the Gateway of the One Mind, but all who reach this gate fear to enter. I do NOT teach a doctrine of extinction! Few understand this, but those who do understand are the only ones to become Buddhas. Treasure this gem!

*   *   *

55. Q: But how can we prevent ourselves from falling into the error of making distinctions between this and that?

A: By realizing that, though you eat the whole day through, no single grain has passed your lips; and that a day's journey has not taken you a single step forward—also by uniformly abstaining from such notions as 'self' and 'other'. DO NOT PERMIT THE EVENTS OF YOUR DAILY LIVES TO BIND YOU, BUT NEVER WITHDRAW YOURSELVES FROM THEM. Only by acting thus can you earn the title of 'A Liberated One'.

Never allow yourselves to mistake outward appearance for reality. Avoid the error of thinking in terms of past, present and future. The past has not gone; the present is a fleeting moment; the future is not yet to come. When you practise mind-control,[2] sit in the proper position, stay perfectly tranquil, and do not permit the least movement of your minds to disturb you. This alone is what is called liberation.[3]

Ah, be diligent! Be diligent! Of a thousand or ten

---

[1] Taoist.
[2] Zazen or dhyāna.
[3] From the burden of ever-renewed transitory existence.

thousand attempting to enter by this Gate, only three or perhaps five pass through. If you are heedless of my warnings, calamity is sure to follow. Therefore is it written:

> Exert your strength in THIS life to attain!
> Or else incur long aeons of further gain!

*   *   *

56. The Master passed away on this mountain during the T'ai Chung Reign (A.D. 847-859) of the T'ang Dynasty. The Emperor Hsüan Tsung bestowed upon him the posthumous title of 'The Zen Master Who Destroys All Limitations'. The memorial pagoda is known as 'The Tower of Spacious Karma'.

INDEX